JUSTICE LEAGUE 3000
VOL. 2: THE CAMELOT WAR

JUSTICE LEAGUE 3000

VOLUME 2
THE CAMELOT WAR

KEITH **GIFFEN** J.M. **DEMATTEIS** writers

HOWARD **PORTER**
CHRIS **BATISTA** LEBEAU **UNDERWOOD**
artists

HI-FI colorist

TAYLOR **ESPOSITO** ROB **LEIGH** letterers

HOWARD **PORTER** cover artist

SUPERMAN created by JERRY **SIEGEL** and JOE **SHUSTER**
By special arrangement with the Jerry **Siegel** family

HARVEY RICHARDS Editor – Original Series PAUL SANTOS Editor
ROBBIN BROSTERMAN Design Director – Books ROBBIE BIEDERMAN – Publication Design

BOB HARRAS Senior VP – Editor-in-Chief, DC Comics

JUSTICE LEAGUE 3000 VOL. 2: THE CAMELOT WAR

DC Comics, 1700 Broadway, New York, NY 10019
A Warner Bros. Entertainment Company.
Printed by RR Donnelley, Salem, VA, USA. 3/20/15. First Printing.

ISBN: 978-1-4012-5414-8

Library of Congress Cataloging-in-Publication Data

Giffen, Keith, author.
Justice League 3000. Volume 2, The camelot war / Keith Giffen, J.M. Dematteis, Howard Porter.
pages cm. — (The New 52!)
ISBN 978-1-4012-5414-8 (paperback)
1. Graphic novels. I. DeMatteis, J. M., author. II. Porter, Howard, illustrator. III. Title. IV. Title: Camelot war.
PN6728.J87G5363 2015
741.5'973—dc23
2014049036

CADMUSWORLD...
HOW THE HELL DID THIS HAPPEN?
CADMUS IS THE CLOSEST THING TO HOME THAT WE HAVE IN THE 31ST CENTURY--BUT NOW THAT IT'S BEEN TAKEN OVER BY THE FIVE--
THAT'S WHERE YOU'RE WRONG, SUPERMAN. CADMUS ALWAYS BELONGED TO THE FIVE.
TERRY WAS MANIPULATING US--AND EVERYONE ON THIS PLANET--ALL ALONG.
AT LEAST NOW--OUR ENEMIES ARE OUT IN THE OPEN.
JUSTICE LEAGUE 3000
TURNING POINT!
KEITH GIFFEN: MAKES UP THE STORIES
J.M. DEMATTEIS: PUTS THE WORDS IN THE BUBBLES
HOWARD PORTER: DRAWS THE PRETTY PICTURES
HI-FI: COLORS IN THE PRETTY PICTURES
TAYLOR ESPOSITO: FITS ALL THOSE #$%^! WORDS ON THE PAGE
HARVEY RICHARDS: YELLS AT GIFFEN, DEMATTEIS & PORTER
BRIAN CUNNINGHAM: YELLS AT HARVEY

BEING CAPTURED... HUMILIATED...IS BAD ENOUGH--BUT DID WE HAVE TO LEAVE BARRY'S BODY BEHIND?
HE DESERVES A DECENT BURIAL.
AS SICKENING AS IT WAS SEEING BARRY DIE AGAIN, LANTERN--I HAVE NO DOUBT HE'LL BE BACK. THE WONDER TWINS RESURRECTED HIM ONCE--
--AND I'M SURE THEY'LL DO IT AGAIN.
THERE ARE NO "TWINS" ANYMORE, BATMAN. TERI'S DEAD. MURDERED BY HER OWN BROTHER.
I STILL CAN'T WRAP MY HEAD AROUND THAT. HOW COULD TERRY TURN ON HIS OWN FLESH AND BLOOD--?
WHAT KIND OF PERSON DOES THAT?
THE TRUTH IS WE DON'T REALLY KNOW ANYTHING ABOUT HIM. HE MIGHT VERY WELL BE AN--
YOU!
THAT'S ENOUGH TALKING!
NOW SHUT YOUR DAMN MOUTH AND KEEP MOVING!
OOO. THAT WAS A MISTAKE.
Y'THINK?
K'RAAAAASHH

WELL DONE, WONDER WOMAN! THE MORON DESERVED IT!
AS FOR THE REST OF YOU: STAND DOWN. THESE LEGENDARY HEROES AREN'T OUR ENEMIES--
--THEY'RE OUR HONORED GUESTS.
WELCOME HOME, JUSTICE LEAGUE.
"HONORED GUESTS," TERRY?
THEY'VE ALL GOT MICRO-MINIATURE EXPLOSIVES IMPLANTED IN THEIR CELLS. I DON'T SEE ANY HONOR IN THAT.
SPOKEN LIKE THE FIERCELY PROTECTIVE MOTHER YOU ARE, ARIEL. I WOULDN'T EXPECT ANY LESS OF YOU.
BUT REST ASSURED THAT THE MICRO-MINES ARE SIMPLY A MEANS TO AN END. WHEN I HAVE A CHANCE TO TALK WITH YOU ALL...EXPLAIN THINGS--

--I SUSPECT YOU'LL BE JOINING ME OF YOUR OWN FREE WILL. THESE OTHER... INDUCEMENTS WILL BE UNNECESSARY.
COEVAL ALREADY TRIED TO RECRUIT US--AND HE FAILED.
NOT COMPLETELY.
WHAT ARE YOU TALKING ABOUT?
HE'S TALKING ABOUT ME.
YOU SEE... COEVAL MADE ME AN OFFER I COULDN'T REFUSE.
YOU BETRAYED US?
THERE'S NO "US" TO BETRAY, DIANA.
MAYBE I WAS PART OF THE LEAGUE ONCE...A THOUSAND YEARS AGO...BUT IT'S A NEW WORLD NOW--
--AND FIRESTORM HAS TO LOOK OUT FOR HIMSELF!
AND AS LONG AS YOUR INTERESTS AND MINE INTERSECT, I THINK IT WILL BE A MUTUALLY BENEFICIAL ARRANGEMENT.
HOW COULD YOU DO IT? THE LEAGUE IS A FAMILY! WE'RE--
A FAMILY? PLEASE! YOU FOUR CAN BARELY TOLERATE EACH OTHER!
WHEN THE TWINS REBOOTED US, OUR MINDS WERE DAMAGED...OUR MEMORIES WERE FRAGMENTED. FACE IT, HAL: THE PEOPLE WE WERE BEFORE ARE LONG DEAD--
--AND OUR LOYALTIES DIED WITH THEM.
ALL I'M DOING FOR TERRY IS THE OCCASIONAL FREELANCE GIG. THE REST OF THE TIME--I'M MY OWN MAN, CHARTING MY OWN DESTINY.
A SIMPLE-- AND ELEGANT-- AGREEMENT. ONE I'D BE DELIGHTED TO OFFER ANY OF YOU.
CAN I GO NOW?
"BY ALL MEANS.
"AND BE SURE TO LET US KNOW HOW YOUR FIRST MISSION GOES."

IN THE TARKOVSKY SECTOR. SOME NUCLEAR FIREWORKS SHOULD PUT AN END TO THAT.
FUNNY. I WAS SURE YOU'D BE THE ONE TO SELL US OUT, CLARK.
REALLY? I ALWAYS THOUGHT IT'D BE YOU. HELL, EVEN BACK IN THE DAY YOU WERE A DUPLICITOUS, MANEUVERING--
YOU TWO CAN INSULT EACH OTHER LATER. NOW MOVE ALONG--
--OR WILL I HAVE TO DETONATE ANOTHER ONE OF YOU...?
AND THAT'S HOW YOU TREAT YOUR "HONORED GUESTS"?
ONLY WHEN FORCED TO.
YOU'RE A MONSTER, TERRY--AND I CAN'T BELIEVE I NEVER SAW IT.
YOU CREATED THIS WORLD, ARIEL... WE'RE ALL JUST DOING THE BEST WE CAN TO SURVIVE IN IT.
I SHOULDN'T HAVE RUN. IF I'D STAYED, I MIGHT HAVE BEEN ABLE TO STOP THE PROJECT--
--AND YOU ALONG WITH IT.
DOUBTFUL. YOU'VE BEEN HAILED AS A GENIUS, A VISIONARY--
--BUT NEXT TO ME YOU'RE A MENTAL DEFECTIVE. NOW MOVE--
--OR I'LL KILL EVERY ONE OF YOU WHERE YOU STAND.
THAT'S IT! I'VE HAD ENOUGH OF--
WHY BOTHER?

"THERE'S NO WAY OUT."
...YOU HAVEN'T TOUCHED YOUR DINNER.
I'M NOT HUNGRY.
YOU SHOULD BE--
--AFTER SITTING IN A CELL FOR THREE DAYS.
AND IT'S DURLAN STEW. TERI'S FAVORITE. SHE LOVED THE WAY THE FLAVORS KEPT CHANGING AND--
YOUR SISTER, TERRY. WHY?
I LOVED HER...I REALLY DID.
CADMUS
BUT SHE HAD MY FATHER'S CONSCIENCE--AND HIS BLEEDING HEART.
IF I'D TOLD HER WHAT I WAS DOING, SHE WOULD HAVE TURNED AGAINST ME IN A HEARTBEAT. SO YOU SEE--
--I HAD NO CHOICE.
THERE'S ALWAYS A CHOICE.
LIKE THE CHOICE YOU MADE WHEN YOU ABANDONED US?
I DID WHAT WAS RIGHT.
NO. YOU WERE AFRAID--OF YOUR OWN POWER...YOUR OWN GREATNESS.
YOU BROUGHT THE PROJECT INTO BEING, ARIEL! YOU INSPIRED US ALL! AND THEN--JUST WHEN SUCCESS WAS WITHIN REACH--YOU GAVE IN TO FEAR.
AND NOW...I'LL HAVE TO USE THAT FEAR AGAINST YOU.
I'VE ALREADY KILLED THE FLASH--AND THE ENTIRE CADMUS STAFF.

THOSE HALLS ARE THICK WITH THE BLOOD AND BONES OF PEOPLE YOU KNEW INTIMATELY. ALL OF THEM SEEDED WITH MICRO-MINES.
HOW MANY MORE WILL DIE BEFORE YOU AGREE TO CONTINUE YOUR WORK HERE--
--AND SERVE A MAN WHO'S PROVEN HIMSELF YOUR MASTER?
YOU'RE NOT A MAN, TERRY.
YOU'RE JUST A DISTURBED LITTLE BOY.
I'M WARNING YOU, ARIEL! TALK TO ME LIKE THAT AGAIN AND--
AND WHAT? THERE ARE NO MINES EMBEDDED IN MY CELLS.
NO. BUT ONE MORE WORD AND YOUR PRECIOUS JUSTICE LEAGUE WILL BE DEAD. AGAIN.
AND THEN I'LL REVIVE THEM. AND KILL THEM. AND REVIVE THEM. AND KILL THEM. OVER AND OVER AND OVER.
UNTIL
YOU
AGREE.
ALL RIGHT.
EXCELLENT! I KNEW YOUR MATERNAL INSTINCTS WOULD WIN OUT IN THE END.
I'M NOT THEIR MOTHER.
OH, BUT YOU ARE! MOTHER TO THE JUSTICE LEAGUE--
--AND MOTHER TO A NEW AGE!
I THINK YOU'LL LIKE THE WORLD I'M CREATING, ARIEL. IT MAY BE A TRIFLE... UGLY GETTING THERE--
--BUT

"IT WILL BE GLORIOUS!"
...SO YOU'RE TELLING ME THAT THIS VAULT IS STOCKED WITH D.N.A.? AND ALL OF THE SAMPLES COME FROM METAHUMANS OF THE 21ST CENTURY?
97.6% OF THE SUPER-HERO COMMUNITY, ACCORDING TO TERRY.
RUMOR IS CADMUS ONCE HAD AN ENTIRE ISLAND DEVOTED TO THIS RESEARCH.
SHUT IT, CONVERT: I DON'T GIVE A RAT'S ASS ABOUT THAT!
WHAT I WANT IS FOR MASTERS TO WHIP ME UP AN ENTIRE HAREM OF HAL JORDANS! SIX OR EIGHT TO START AND THEN--
LOCUS-- WHAT IS THIS OBSESSION WITH GREEN LANTERN?
IT'S NOT AN OBSESSION: IT'S TRUE LOVE!
YOU WOULDN'T RECOGNIZE TRUE LOVE IF IT BIT YOU ON THE--
SPU-LOOO

...THAT BITCH!
IT'S THE PRINCIPLE OF THE THING!
PLEASE, CONVERT. YOU'VE GOT BODIES EVERY-WHERE.
WHY ARE YOU COMPLAINING ABOUT LOSING ONE?
LOCUS DOESN'T HAVE PRINCIPLES.
MY POINT EXACTLY.
LET HER HAVE HER FUN IN THE D.N.A. VAULT. YOU'RE MORE USE TO US HERE--IN THAT SECURITY CHIEF'S BODY.
AND A LOVELY BODY IT IS.
YOU CAN PLAY WITH IT LATER.
RIGHT NOW I NEED YOU TO MAKE SURE THAT I'M UPLOADED INTO CADMUS'S SYSTEMS.
I THOUGHT TERRY HELPED YOU BREACH CADMUS MONTHS AGO.
THOSE WERE COVERT STRIKES. NOW WE NEED FULL INTEGRATION.
I WANT TO MONITOR EVERY-THING ARIEL MASTERS DOES. IT'S ONLY A MATTER OF TIME NOW TILL SHE ADDRESSES THE FLAWS IN THE RESURRECTION PROTOCOLS.
I OBSERVE THE PROCESS ONCE--
--AND I CAN REPLICATE IT FOREVER.
AND MASTERS...?

"--WILL HAVE OUTLIVED HER OWN USEFULNESS."
...YOU DO REALIZE THAT ONCE MASTERS FINISHES HER WORK, WE BECOME EXPENDABLE.
WE'VE BEEN EXPENDABLE FROM DAY ONE, HAL.
I'M SURPRISED THEY HAVEN'T EXECUTED US ALREADY. WE'VE BEEN LOCKED UP HERE IN OUR QUARTERS FOR OVER A WEEK NOW.
OH, THEY'LL KILL US ALL RIGHT. IF ARIEL PERFECTS THE PROCESS--
NOT IF... WHEN.
WHEN SHE PERFECTS THE PROCESS--TERRY'S NOT GOING TO NEED FIVE FLAWED CLONES AROUND.
WE'RE NOT CLONES, HAL--ALTHOUGH GOD KNOWS I WISH WE WERE.
SORRY. YOU THREE HAVE HAD SOME TIME TO ADJUST TO THE TRUTH ABOUT OUR ORIGINS--
--BUT I JUST FOUND OUT AND--
TRUST ME--TIME DOESN'T MAKE IT ANY EASIER TO ACCEPT.
INNOCENT PEOPLE DYING SO THAT WE CAN LIVE? OUR D.N.A. OVERWRITING THEIRS?
IT'S... DISGUSTING.
TO SAY THE LEAST.
WHICH IS WHY WE'VE GOT TO GET THE HELL OUT OF HERE--AND THEN FIND A WAY TO BRING THIS PLACE DOWN.
YOU DO KNOW WE'RE BEING MONITORED...?
WE'LL STOP THEM, BRUCE. I PROMISE YOU.
SAID THE MAN WHO'S SIX INCHES TALL AND HIDING IN HIS OWN POCKET.
UNTIL I CAN FIND A WAY TO UNDO WHAT LOCUS DID TO ME--
--USING AN ENERGY CONSTRUCT SEEMS THE BEST WAY TO GO.
AND WHAT ABOUT THE FACT THAT YOUR OWN POWER IS POISONING YOU?

LOCUS DESTROYED YOUR DAMPING CLOAK, DIDN'T SHE? WHICH MEANS THE GREEN CANCER IS EATING AWAY AT YOUR CELLS--
I GRABBED ONE OF THE SPARES IN MY QUARTERS. SHOULD DO THE TRICK.
EVEN WITH THE DAMN CLOAK, EVERY TIME YOU USE THE EMERALD ENERGY, YOU'RE ONE STEP CLOSER TO DEATH.
WE'RE ALL DANCING WITH DEATH EVERY DAY.
IT'S JUST A LITTLE MORE OBVIOUS FOR ME.
YEAH, WELL, MAYBE DEATH IS THE BEST OPTION FOR ALL OF US.
WHAT'RE YOU TALKING ABOUT? WE'RE HEROES. WE'VE GOT A JOB TO DO AND--
WE WERE HEROES...ONCE! WE FOUGHT THE GOOD FIGHT, DAY AFTER DAY, AND IN THE END--WE DIED FOR THE CAUSE.
BUT I DON'T RECALL ANYONE ASKING ME IF I WANTED TO COME BACK AND DO IT AGAIN!
WE GAVE THE WORLD EVERYTHING, HAL, AND NOW--
NOW WE'RE GOING TO DO IT ONE MORE TIME--
--BECAUSE THAT'S WHO WE ARE.
I HOPE TO GOD YOU'RE RIGHT.
OF COURSE I AM. NOW, C'MON--YOU USED TO PRIDE YOURSELF ON BEING AN ESCAPE ARTIST--
--HELP ME COOK UP A PLAN TO--

ESCAPE? SINCE THEY REVIVED US WE'VE DONE NOTHING BUT TRIP OVER OUR OWN FEET!
WHAT MAKES YOU THINK WE'RE CAPABLE OF ENGINEERING A BREAKOUT?
AND WHAT'S THE ALTERNATIVE?
SIT AROUND HERE LIKE GOOD LITTLE LAMBS--WAITING FOR THEM TO SLAUGHTER US...OR BRAINWASH US... OR WORSE?
DIANA, PRINCESS OF THEMYSCIRA, IS NOBODY'S "LITTLE LAMB"!
BUT I AM A REALIST: WE'RE UNDER ROUND-THE-CLOCK SURVEILLANCE!
THERE'S NO WAY WE CAN HATCH AN ESCAPE PLAN WITH TERRY AND HIS GOONS WATCHING OUR EVERY--
REALLY? SEEM T'ME WE'VE BEEN TALKING ESCAPE FOR A WHILE NOW. SO WHY HAVEN'T THE ALARMS GONE OFF?
WHY HAVEN'T THE STORM TROOPERS COME MARCHING IN?
YOU DID SOME-THING--
--DIDN'T YOU...?
MAYBE.
KEEP THIS UP, JORDAN--

--AND I JUST MAY
TART BELIEVING IN
HEROES AGAIN."
...YOU DID WHAT?
BYPASSED THE SECURITY SYSTEM AND ALTERED THE SURVEILLANCE SO THAT TERRY'S GUARD DOGS ONLY HEAR WHAT I WANT THEM TO HEAR.
THAT'S PRETTY COMPLEX, EVEN FOR A GL. HOW'D YOU DO IT?
THAT'S THE WEIRD PART: I DON'T REALLY KNOW.
WHAT DO YOU MEAN YOU DON'T KNOW?
I JUST KIND OF...THOUGHT ABOUT IT AND IT HAPPENED.
USUALLY THIS KIND OF THING REQUIRES INTENSE FOCUS. WILL PLUS IMAGINATION EQUALS MANIFESTATION. THAT'S THE WAY IT WORKS FOR LANTERNS.
BUT THIS TIME? I HAD A RANDOM THOUGHT AND-- BINGO.
THAT'S KIND OF CREEPY.
I HATE TO AGREE WITH CLARK--
DON'T CALL ME CLARK!
--BUT HE HAS A POINT.
AGREED. THIS IS ONE RANDOM THOUGHT THAT HAD A BENEFICIAL OUTCOME--
--BUT WHEN YOU CONSIDER THE FARRAGO OF CONTRADICTORY--AND DANGEROUS--IMPULSES THAT SWIM THROUGH A HUMAN MIND IN THE COURSE OF A DAY--!
GO OVER IT AGAIN.
THERE'S REALLY NOTHING TO GO OVER.
I WAS JUST WISHING WE COULD FIND A WAY TO OVERRIDE TERRY'S SURVEILLANCE SYSTEM WHEN, ALL OF A SUDDEN--
--I WAS IN THE SYSTEM-- IMMERSED IN IT...ONE WITH IT...JUST LIKE COEVAL! AND, WITHOUT KNOWING HOW, I JUST...CHANGED IT.
SO YOU'RE...WHAT? ALADDIN AND THE GENIE? YOU MAKE A WISH AND THE GREEN ENERGY INSTANTLY GRANTS IT...?
NO EFFORT REQUIRED?
IF HE CAN LEARN TO DO THIS MORE CONSCIOUSLY, THE POTENTIAL FOR GOOD IS INCALCULABLE.
SO IS THE POTENTIAL FOR DISASTER.

"DISASTER? I JUST HANDED US A GOLDEN TICKET--AND YOU'RE ALL COMPLAINING?"
"WHAT WAS IT LIKE WHEN YOU WERE IN THE SYSTEM? GO THROUGH IT STEP BY STEP."
"I DON'T OWE YOU ANY EXPLANATIONS, BRUCE--BUT I'LL TELL YOU ANYWAY.
"IT WAS A VIRTUAL WORLD--
"--LIKE THE ONE YOU WERE ALL IMMERSED IN WHEN COEVAL INTERROGATED YOU BACK ON IDYLL.
"I COULD FEEL THE GREEN ENERGY CARRYING ME ALONG, FASTER THAN THOUGHT... ALMOST AS IF IT HAD A LIFE AND WILL OF ITS OWN--
"--AND IT BROUGHT ME TO THE SECURITY NEXUS--
"--WHERE IT OVERLAID PAST IMAGES FROM OUR TIME AT CADMUS OVER THE CURRENT FEED.
"ANYONE CHECKS IN ON US, ALL THEY'LL SEE IS US MOPING AROUND, ARGUING--AND COMPLAINING ABOUT THE FOOD."
"HEY! I LIKE THE FOOD!
IT'S SYNTHETIC PROTEIN PASTE!
YEAH, BUT IT'S YUMMY SYNTHETIC PROTEIN PASTE!
I'M ESPECIALLY FOND OF THE VEGETABLE BIRYANI PASTE. IT ALWAYS HITS THE SPO--
CAN WE GET BACK ON POINT, PLEASE?
WHAT IS THE POINT?
WHEN THEY RESURRECTED ME--THEY MUST HAVE USED 30TH CENTURY TECH TO RAMP UP MY POWER.
YOU'RE THE PERFECT WEAPON TO USE AGAINST THEM--AND THEY CREATED YOU!
I DON'T KNOW HOW PERFECT I AM--BUT I DO KNOW THAT...WHILE THEY'RE WATCHING THE FEED OF BRUCE AND CLARK ENDLESSLY ANTAGONIZING EACH OTHER...THE FOUR US CAN JUST--
WALK RIGHT OUT OF HERE...?

"PRECISELY!"
EXCUSE ME?
TERRY'S LET YOU HAVE FREE REIN HERE IN THE D.N.A. VAULTS--AND I THINK IT'S A SERIOUS MISTAKE.
I'LL MAKE A NOTE OF THAT IN MY DIARY, CONVERT.
WHY HE'S ALLOWING YOU TO HAVE THIS LEVEL OF FREEDOM IS--
FREEDOM?!
WHAT ARE YOU UP TO, MASTERS?
BEING FORCED TO BEND TO THAT BASTARD'S WILL IN ORDER TO SPARE INNOCENT LIVES? YOU CALL THAT FREEDOM?
I CALL IT SOUL-CRUSHING SLAVERY!
IF YOU WANT TO SEE SLAVERY, MASTERS--YOU SHOULD STUDY SOME OF THE STAR SYSTEMS THE FIVE HAVE CONQUERED. BELIEVE ME, NEXT TO THEM--
--YOU'RE LIVING IN PARADISE.
YOU'RE RIGHT TO BE SUSPICIOUS OF ME, CONVERT--BECAUSE THE FIRST CHANCE I GET, I'LL DO EVERYTHING IN MY POWER TO BRING THE FIVE DOWN--
--IN A BALL OF FIRE.
TRY, ARIEL. PLEASE TRY. IT WILL GIVE ME AN EXCUSE TO EXTINGUISH YOUR PATHETIC LIFE FROM THE INSIDE OUT.
JUST IMAGINE THE THINGS I'LL DO WHEN I FINALLY TAKE POSSESSION OF YOUR BODY.
NOT YET, YOU BLOODTHIRSTY ANIMAL. TERRY WANTS ME ALIVE.
INDEED HE DOES.
BUT OUR TERRY IS A...CAPRICIOUS SORT. AND ONE OF THESE DAYS...SOON, I HOPE...HE'LL CHANGE HIS MIND AND YOU WILL, QUITE LITERALLY--
804-T2

"--BELONG TO ME."
...WE'VE BEEN TRYING TO GET WORD TO YOU FOR DAYS NOW.
BRUCE...?
WHERE HAVE YOU BEEN?
WHERE HAVE YOU BEEN?
LOCKED AWAY IN THE VAULTS... DANCING TO TERRY'S TUNE.
WELL, YOU MAY NOT HAVE TO DANCE MUCH LONGER. GREEN LANTERN HAS--
BE CAREFUL WHAT YOU SAY. COEVAL'S BEEN MONITORING ME.
WHAT HE DOESN'T KNOW IS THAT I'VE BEEN MONITORING HIM IN RETURN--
--AND RIGHT NOW HE SEEMS TO BE OFF THE GRID... PROBABLY BUSY WITH TERRY--
--BUT HE COULD COME BACK ON AT ANY MOMENT.

HAL MAY BE ABLE TO HELP WITH THAT. YOU SEE, HE--
I DON'T NEED HAL.
WHAT ARE YOU TALKING ABOUT?
I'VE FOUND THE SOLUTION TO OUR PROBLEM...AND SHE'S BEEN UNDER OUR NOSES THE WHOLE TIME!
"SHE"?
TERI.
YOU MEAN YOU'VE DONE IT? PERFECTED THE RESURRECTION PROCESS AND--
YOU STILL DON'T GET IT, DO YOU?
THERE IS NO WAY TO PERFECT IT!
WHAT?
THERE IS NO WAY TO PERFECT IT.
BUT TERRY THINKS YOU CAN--
I KNOW WHAT TERRY THINKS--
--AND HE'S WRONG.
BUT YOU SAID YOU FOUND THE SOLUTION AND THAT SHE--
OH, NO.
ARIEL--

"--WHAT HAVE YOU DONE?"
...THAT'S MY SISTER.
YES, IT IS.
SHE REPLICATED MY SISTER...?
YOU TOLD US TO LET HER DO AS SHE PLEASED--
AND SHE USED--
--THE SAME PROCEDURE EMPLOYED TO RESURRECT THE JUSTICE LEAGUE.
A LIVING DONOR?
YES.
SO DESPITE ALL OF ARIEL'S PROTESTATIONS ABOUT THE LOSS OF INNOCENT LIFE--
--SHE'S STILL WILLING TO MAKE THE NECESSARY SACRIFICES IF THE CAUSE IS JUST.
SHE'S UP TO SOMETHING.
I DON'T THINK SO. ARIEL'S NOTHING IF NOT EFFICIENT. IF SHE'S REPLICATED TERI, THERE'S A DAMN GOOD REASON.
AND IF THAT REASON ISN'T TO OUR BENEFIT?
SHE WOULDN'T DARE. THERE ARE TOO MANY LIVES AT STAKE. ARIEL KNOWS I WOULDN'T HESITATE TO DESTROY AN ENTIRE SOLAR SYSTEM JUST TO PUNISH HER.
AND OF COURSE I'D IGNITE THE IMPLANTS IN HER PRECIOUS JUSTICE LEAGUE...AND THEY'D ALL GO PFFFT--
KLIK
KLIK
KLIK
SHE DIDN'T HESITATE TO USE THE DONOR. THAT MAKES HER A MURDERER. AND, AS MURDERERS OURSELVES, WE KNOW THAT--
--JUST LIKE THE FLASH.
SHE HAS NOWHERE TO GO. SHE'S OURS--AND SHE KNOWS IT.
TRUST ME, COEVAL: ARIEL WILL GIVE ME WHAT I WANT.
SHE HAS NO CHOICE.
THERE ARE ALWAYS CHOICES. YOU, ABOVE ALL--

"--SHOULD KNOW THAT."
...ARIEL? ARIEL--WHAT HAPPENED? I--
YOU WERE DEAD, TERI. BUT THANKS TO ME--
--YOU'RE BACK.
I REMEMBER TALKING TO YOU ALL ON THE MONITORS AND THEN--
I CAN'T REMEMBER--!
WE'LL...AH...GET TO HOW YOU DIED LATER. RIGHT NOW I WANT TO DISCUSS--
--THE MODIFICATIONS I MADE TO YOUR D.N.A.
MODIFICATIONS? WHAT ARE YOU--
I DON'T HAVE TIME TO EXPLAIN. COEVAL WILL BE BACK ON THE GRID ANY TIME NOW.
COEVAL'S HERE? AT CADMUS? I DON'T UNDERSTAND!
YOU AND THE OTHERS HAD ESCAPED IDYLL. YOU WERE ON A RIMWORLD WHEN--
WITH ALL DUE RESPECT, TERI--THERE'S NO DAMN TIME FOR THIS. YOUR GEAR'S IN THE BACK. PUT IT ON BEFORE--
BUT--
DO IT! NOW!
I HOPE TO GOD HAL'S GOT THIS COVERED.
IT WON'T LAST LONG. COEVAL'S BOUND TO DISCOVER WHAT YOU'RE UP TO AND--
DON'T YOU THINK I KNOW THAT?
DAMMIT, BRUCE--I SACRIFICED A HUMAN LIFE SO THAT WE'D HAVE A FIGHTING CHANCE--
--AND I'LL HAVE TO LIVE WITH THAT CHOICE...WITH THAT GHOST... FOREVER!
BUT IF IT MEANS TAKING DOWN THE FIVE AND SPARING OTHER INNOCENT LIVES, THEN--
THE INSTANT THEY GET A LOCK ON TERI, THEY'LL KNOW YOU'VE BEEN PLAYING THEM.
I KNOW. AND THAT'S WHY--

--WE HAVE TO MOVE FAST.
UH... ARIEL--
--IS THERE SOMETHING I SHOULD KNOW?

CADMUSWORLD...
YOU'VE TAKEN A HUGE RISK, ARIEL: RESURRECTING TERI... FUSING HER D.N.A. WITH BARRY'S AND TURNING HER INTO A NEW INCARNATION OF THE FLASH--
DESPERATE TIMES, BATMAN.
HOW WILL WE KNOW IF HER MISSION SUCCEEDS?
EASY--
--YOU WON'T EXPLODE.
JUSTICE LEAGUE 3000
BREAKOUT!
GIFFEN & DEMATTEIS STORY
HOWARD PORTER ART HI-FI COLORS
TAYLOR ESPOSITO LETTERS
BRIAN CUNNINGHAM AUTHORITY FIGURE
HARVEY RICHARDS EDITOR

IT'S UNSETTLING--TO SAY THE LEAST--KNOWING THAT THERE ARE MICRO-MINES IMPLANTED IN OUR CELLS.
WELL, IF WE GET OFF CADMUSWORLD IN ONE PIECE, I'M SURE I CAN FIND A WAY TO NEUTRALIZE THEM. BUT TILL THEN, THE JUSTICE LEAGUE'S FATE--
--IS IN THE FLASH'S HANDS.
WHY DIDN'T YOU BRING BARRY BACK? WHY USE TERI INSTEAD?
I NEEDED SOME-ONE WHO KNEW CADMUS... KNEW TERRY...AND WHO'D BE FAST ENOUGH TO GET TO HIM BEFORE HE KEYED THE DETONATORS.
I'M ALSO COUNTING ON TERI'S RAGE. HER BROTHER... THE ONE PERSON SHE TRUSTED IN ALL THE WORLD...MURDERED HER. THAT'S GOT TO STING.
RAGE IS AN EXCELLENT MOTIVATOR.
AND THE TRUTH IS, POOR BARRY HAD JUST BEEN KILLED...AGAIN... AND I DIDN'T HAVE THE HEART TO--
OH, STOP PRETENDING, ARIEL: YOU HAVE NO HEART.
I THOUGHT YOU WENT AFTER THE FLASH, COEVAL.
I'M A SENTIENT COMPUTER PROGRAM: I'M NOT LIMITED BY LOCATION. I CAN BE ANYWHERE... AND EVERYWHERE.
AND YET I MANAGED TO TRANSFORM TERI...RIGHT UNDER YOUR CYBERNATED NOSE.
BET TERRY'S NOT VERY HAPPY ABOUT THAT.
SILENCE, WOMAN, BEFORE I--
SPARE US THE THREATS. IF YOU WERE GOING TO KILL US--
--YOU'D HAVE DONE IT ALREADY.
WHICH MEANS TERI'S ALREADY GOT HER BROTHER IN A DEATH GRIP--AND YOU HAVE NO CHOICE BUT TO STEP ASIDE--
--AND LET US WALK OUT OF HERE.
IT'S NOT GOING TO BE THAT EASY.
I THINK IT WILL BE.

I DON'T UNDERSTAND YOU, MASTERS: YOU TRAINED THE TWINS. BIRTHED THIS PROJECT.
AND WALKED AWAY FROM IT.
IN THE NAME OF MORALITY?
YES.
AND WHERE WAS YOUR MORALITY WHEN YOU RESURRECTED TERI? SUBJECTED ANOTHER "VOLUNTEER" TO YOUR D.N.A. OVERRIDE PROCESS?
I DID--
--WHAT HAD TO BE DONE.
I'M SURE TERRY WOULD SAY THE SAME THING.
WE'RE LEAVING, COEVAL. NOW.
I'D ADVISE YOU TO STAY OUT OF OUR WAY. FOR TERRY'S SAKE--
--AND YOUR OWN.
I'LL DO WHATEVER TERRY ASKS OF ME. BUT I CAN'T PROMISE THE SAME--
--FOR LOCUS.
SHE'S MAD AS THE PROVERBIAL HATTER--WITH A MIND THAT CAN BEND REALITY.
AND SHE'S GOT A RATHER... UNHEALTHY OBSESSION WITH YOUR GREEN-HUED FRIEND.
WHEN SHE DISCOVERS THAT HER PRECIOUS GREEN LANTERN IS LEAVING--
--WHY, THERE'S NO TELLING WHAT SHE'LL DO.
SHE MIGHT TURN THE JUSTICE LEAGUE INTO FINGER PUPPETS OR POTTED PLANTS. OR JUST WIPE YOU ALL OUT OF EXISTENCE--
--WITH A SINGLE THOUGHT.
HE'S RIGHT, YOU KNOW.
LET'S CROSS THAT BRIDGE WHEN WE GET TO IT.

"--TERI CAN'T HOLD THEM OFF FOREVER."
...TRANSVERSAL CHECKS OUT--AND I'VE TARGETED A WORLD FAR BEYOND THE RANGE OF THE DETONATION SIGNAL--
I DON'T LIKE RUNNING FROM A FIGHT.
ME NEITHER. BUT IT BEATS THE HELL OUT OF BLOWING UP FROM THE INSIDE OUT.
AND ONCE WE'RE GONE--WHAT'S TO STOP TERRY FROM USING OUR D.N.A. TO CREATE AN ENTIRE ARMY OF JUSTICE LEAGUES TO COME AFTER US?
WELL, THAT'S A DEPRESSING THOUGHT.
LET'S JUST GO, ALL RIGHT?
EVERY SINGLE ONE OF THESE PEOPLE IS THE CONVERT. AND I DON'T TRUST ANY OF THEM.
WONDER WOMAN'S RIGHT, YOU KNOW. THERE'S NO TELLING WHAT TERRY CAN DO WITH THE CADMUS D.N.A. VAULTS AT HIS DISPOSAL.
AND DON'T TELL ME WE'LL CROSS THAT BRIDGE WHEN WE GET TO IT.
IS THERE ANY OTHER CHOICE?
NO.
BEEP BEEP BEEP BEEP
THEN LOCK AND LOAD.
DONE! COORDINATES ARE SET AND THE TRANSVERSAL'S PROGRAMMED TO SELF-DESTRUCT ONCE WE'RE ON THE OTHER--

WHERE THE HELL DO YOU THINK YOU'RE GOING?!
:SIGH: IF THERE IS A GOD--
--I DON'T THINK HE LIKES US VERY MUCH.
THE ONLY GOD AROUND HERE--
--IS LOCUS!
AND I SWEAR TO ME THAT--IF I DIDN'T NEED THAT BITCH ARIEL TO HELP ME MAKE MY GREEN LANTERN HAREM--
--I'D VAPORIZE THE LOT OF YOU!
"GREEN LANTERN HAREM"?
THAT'S RIGHT, HALLY! I'M GOING TO USE YOUR D.N.A. TO MAKE DOZENS OF YOU...NO, HUNDREDS!
ONE FOR EVERY NIGHT OF THE YEAR!
BUT I CAN'T DO IT WITHOUT MASTERS' HELP!
WAIT A MINUTE. CAN'T SHE JUST USE HER MIND TO--
SHHH! SHE HASN'T REALIZED THAT YET!
NO TALKING! I WANT ARIEL DOWN IN THE VAULT AND EVERYONE ELSE BACK IN THEIR QUARTERS OR I'LL--
LOCUS... FOR ONCE IN YOUR LIFE WOULD YOU JUST--
--SHUT UP?!

HAL--WHAT ARE YOU *DOING?* IF YOU *ANTAGONIZE* LOCUS, SHE'LL--

LOOK, SHE *CLEARLY* DOESN'T CARE IF TERRY LIVES OR DIES--WHICH MEANS SHE'S CAPABLE OF *ANYTHING!*

ALL THE MORE REASON FOR US TO TAKE HER ON *TOGETHER!*

NO! I'M THE ONE SHE'S FOCUSED ON--SO IT SHOULD BE EASY ENOUGH TO KEEP HER *BUSY* WHILE YOU--

WE'RE *NOT* LEAVING YOU BEHIND!

I DIDN'T GIVE YOU A CHOICE!

HAL-- *NO!* YOU CAN'T!

YOU BRING THEM BACK HERE *RIGHT NOW!*

HRRRMMMMMMMMMM
SON OF A--!
FZZAAKKK
HE HAD NO RIGHT TO DO THAT! NO RIGHT!
WHERE ARE WE, ARIEL?
HALFWAY ACROSS THE UNIVERSE-- IN ONE OF MY HIDDEN LABS.
THE TRANSVERSAL! CAN WE--
BOOM
IT BLEW UP!
THAT WAS THE PLAN, RIGHT? MAKES IT A LITTLE HARDER FOR THEM TO FOLLOW US.
BUT YOU'VE GOT ANOTHER ONE OVER THERE!
YOUR POWERS OF OBSERVATION ARE ASTOUNDING.
THANK YOU! I--
YOU WERE BEING SARCASTIC, WEREN'T YOU?
JUST BE QUIET FOR A MINUTE AND LET ME--
I DEMAND THAT YOU SEND US BACK! NOW!
HAL CAN TAKE CARE OF HIMSELF! THE GREEN ENERGY CAN LEAD HIM HERE AND--
I'M NOT WORRIED ABOUT HAL! I'M WORRIED ABOUT TERI!
GOOD. BECAUSE I AM, TOO. WHICH IS WHY I'M LINKING THIS 'VERSAL UP TO THE SUBORBITAL NETWORK AROUND CADMUSWORLD.
YOU MIGHT HAVE JUST SAID THAT.
BUT I'M NOT RISKING THE ENTIRE LEAGUE ON THIS. ONLY ONE OF YOU IS GOING BACK FOR HER.

"ANY VOLUNTEERS?"
...I URGE RESTRAINT, LOCUS--AS I ALWAYS DO.
AND AS I ALWAYS DO--I REJECT YOUR URGINGS!
BUT THE GREEN ONE IS FAR MORE VALUABLE TO US IF HE'S ALIVE.
WE HAVE THE D.N.A. VAULTS NOW--
--WHAT DO WE NEED HIM FOR?
WE HAVE NOT YET MASTERED THE MYSTERIES OF THE VAULTS. AND HIS EMERALD ENERGY MIGHT BE A VALUABLE AID IN--
DO ME A FAVOR, COEVAL--
--SHUT THE #%&# UP!
YOU WILL REGRET THIS, CHILD!
I DOUBT IT.
AS FOR YOU, HALLY-BOY: I KILLED YOU ONCE AND YOU SOMEHOW MANAGED TO COME BACK. THIS TIME--
--I'LL MAKE SURE IT'S PERMANENT!
NO MORE, LOCUS!
YOU KILLED MY BEST FRIEND. TORTURED AND ABUSED ME. SHRUNK ME DOWN TO THE SIZE OF A CHIPMUNK. YOU'RE ONE SICK, TWISTED PUPPY--
--AND IT'S TIME I PUT YOU DOWN!
PLEASE! I'M A FREAKING GOD! WHAT CAN YOU DO TO--
SHTONK
HEY!
I'VE NEVER BEEN ONE TO REVEL IN

--BUT I'M REALLY GONNA ENJOY THIS!
MUCH TO MY REGRET, LOCUS, I'VE SPENT A LOT OF TIME WITH YOU--
WHIRRRRR
STTOPPP
ENOUGH TO REALIZE THAT YOU'VE GOT TO FOCUS YOUR MIND LIKE A LASER IN ORDER TO MANIPULATE REALITY!
BUT YOU CAN'T FOCUS, CAN YOU--WHEN YOU'RE SPINNING LIKE A LOAD OF WET LAUNDRY IN A DRYER?
OH--AND DON'T WORRY, CONVERT--
SKK-KATA-WUKKATA
--I HAVEN'T FORGOTTEN YOU!

DON'T BOTHER TO GET UP--
--I'LL SEE MYSELF OUT.
REST WELL, BARRY.
AND WHILE HAL JORDAN USES THE GREEN ENERGY TO GET A FIX ON ARIEL MASTERS' LOCATION...
...AN ORBITAL ANSVERSAL DROPS INTO THE UPPER MOSPHERE ABOVE CADMUSWORLD...
HANG IN THERE, TERI--
--SUPERMAN'S ON THE WAY!
WAIT--DON'T BAG AND BOARD THIS ISSUE YET! TURN THE PAGE FOR OUR SPECTACULAR SECOND FEATURE, FEATURING THE ALL-NEW FLASH
AND SUPERMAN!
IN ALL-OUT ACTION FOR THE FIRST TIME!

THIS
IS
IN-
SANE!
NEED FOR SPEED!
GIFFEN & DEMATTEIS: STORY
CHRIS BATISTA: PENCILS
LEBEAU UNDERWOOD: INKS
HI-FI: COLORS
TAYLOR ESPOSITO: LETTERS
BRIAN CUNNINGHAM: MASTER OF ALL HE SURVEYS

ONE MINUTE I'M DEAD-- MURDERED BY MY OWN BROTHER...
...AND THE NEXT I'M RESURRECTED...
TEN MINUTES EARLIER...
...WITH THE POWERS OF THE FLASH!
WHATDIDYOU DOTOME?IDON'T UNDERSTAND!I FEELSOSTRANGE AND--
CENTER YOURSELF. NICE DEEP BREATHS. YOU HAVE TO CONTROL THE SPEED--NOT THE OTHER WAY AROUND.
OKAYOKAYI'LLTRY. BUTYOU'VE...GOTTO TELLME...WHY YOU--
--WHY YOU DID THIS! WHY BRING ME BACK WITH BARRY'S POWERS?
YOU KNOW CADMUS. YOU KNOW YOUR BROTHER. AND WITH THE FLASH'S SPEED AT YOUR DISPOSAL--
--YOU'LL BE ABLE TO DO WHAT NEEDS TO BE DONE.
WHICH IS?
STOP HIM FROM DETONATING THE MICRO-MINES HE EMBEDDED IN OUR CELLS.
TERRY WOULDN'T DO THAT!
RIGHT. AND HE WOULDN'T SNAP YOUR NECK WITH A PUMPKIN-SIZED GRIN ON HIS FACE, EITHER.
I DON'T UNDERSTAND. HE'S MY BROTHER! HE'S--
--A PSYCHOPATH, A SOCIOPATH--AND JUST ABOUT ANY OTHER PATH YOU COULD THINK OF.
THERE'SGOTTOBE MORETOITTHANWEREALIZE! MAYBETHEREALTERRY'SBEEN KIDNAPPEDANDTHISONE'SAN IMPOSTOR! ORMAYBEHE'S ADOUBLEAGENTOR--
HE'S THE LEADER OF THE FIVE--AND HE MURDERED YOU IN COLD BLOOD.
BUT YOU BROUGHT ME BACK, ARIEL--WHICH MEANS YOU PERFECTED THE RESURRECTION PROCESS!
NOT... EXACTLY.

"NOT EXACTLY"? WHAT DOES THAT--
WE'LL TALK ABOUT THIS LATER. RIGHT NOW WE'VE GOT TO ACT.
BATMAN'S RIGHT. ODDS ARE COEVAL'S GETTING SUSPICIOUS. HE'S BEEN MONITORING YOUR REBIRTH VERY CLOSELY--
WHICH MEANS WE'VE GOT MINUTES...AT BEST...BEFORE HE TUMBLES TO WHAT ARIEL'S DONE.
I CAN SEE WHAT SHE'S DONE.
AND, REST ASSURED--
--I'M NOT PLEASED!
GO, TERI!
AND JUST LIKE THAT...
...I WAS GONE.
NOW.
FRANKLY, I'M SURPRISED COEVAL DIDN'T DISCOVER ARIEL'S PLAN SOONER...
...BUT ARROGANCE AND OVERCONFIDENCE CAN BE A DEADLY MIX...
...AS TERRY'S ABOUT TO LEARN.
THEY DID WHAT?
COMBINED YOUR SISTER'S D.N.A. WITH BARRY ALLEN'S AND--
AND I'VE GOT JUST ONE QUESTION FOR YOU... BROTHER!

WHY
DID
YOU
KILL
ME?!

ALL OUR LIVES IT WAS THE TWO OF US...TERRY AND TERI, THE WONDER TWINS--
KRAAAAK
--AGAINST THE WORLD!
MOM ABANDONED US! DAD...GOD BLESS HIM...LOVED US--BUT NEVER REALLY UNDERSTOOD US! AND THEN, AFTER HE DIED--
--ALL WE HAD WAS EACH OTHER!
EVEN HERE AT CADMUS, EVERYONE ELSE LOOKED AT US LIKE WE WERE FREAKS!
OUR INTELLIGENCE FRIGHTENED THEM.
WE FRIGHTENED THEM!
AND I FINALLY UNDERSTAND WHAT IT IS THAT THEY WERE AFRAID OF!
BUT NOW IT'S YOUR TURN TO BE AFRAID--
WUDUP WUDUP WUDUP WUDUP WUDUP WUDUP WUDUP WUDUP WUDUP WUDUP WUDUP WUDUP WUDUP WUDUP WUDUP
--YOU TRAITOROUS, MURDERING BASTARD!
YOU...YOU DO REALIZE...THAT CALLING ME THAT--IMPUGNS YOUR OWN BIRTH, AS WELL...?
SHUT UP, DAMN YOU! SHUT UP BEFORE I--
WHAT THE HELL IS GOING ON HERE?

STAY RIGHT WHERE YOU ARE, CONVERT--
--OR I'LL BREAK YOUR PRECIOUS LEADER'S NECK BEFORE YOU CAN EVEN BLINK.
OH, PLEASE... YOU HAVEN'T GOT THE GUTS.
MAYBE I DIDN'T BEFORE. BUT BEING DEAD CHANGES A PERSON.
WHAT DO YOU WANT?
SAFE PASSAGEOUT OFHEREFOR ARIELANDTHE LEAGUE.
WHAT?
SIGH SAFE PASSAGE OUT OF HERE FOR ARIEL AND THE LEAGUE.
AND IF YOU SO MUCH AS THINK ABOUT DETONATING THOSE MICRO-MINES--
--HAVING YOUR NECK SNAPPED WILL BE THE LEAST OF YOUR PROBLEMS.
YOU'RE SUPPOSED TO HAVE EYES EVERYWHERE, COEVAL! HOW THE HELL DID YOU NOT SEE THIS COMING?
SEEING... AND UNDER-STANDING...ARE NOT ALWAYS THE SAME THING.
HUMAN BEHAVIOR CAN OCCASIONALLY SHATTER THE CAREFULLY STRUCTURED PATTERNS OF LOGIC AND--
IN OTHER WORDS: YOU SCREWED UP. BUT DON'T WORRY--
--I'VE GOT THIS.
YOU COULD FILL THIS ENTIRE COMPLEX WITH YOUR DOPPELGANGERS, CONVERT--AND NONE OF THEM COULD STOP ME.
I'M THE FLASH NOW! THE FASTEST WOMAN ALIVE!
NOT ALIVE FOR LONG...ONCE LOCUS GETS HER HANDS ON YOU.
MAYBE. BUT I GUARANTEE YOU'LL BE DEAD BEFORE I WILL.
YOU'RE ENJOYING THIS...AREN'T YOU?

WHICH MEANS WE'RE MORE ALIKE THAN I EVER REALIZED.
JOIN ME! TOGETHER WE CAN--
PLEASE-- YOU'VE ALREADY KILLED ME. DON'T INSULT ME ON TOP OF IT.
MY APOLOGIES. FOR THE INSULT... IF NOT THE MURDER.

NOW HERE'S THE DEAL: PROVIDE THE LEAGUE WITH CLEAN TRANSVERSAL ACCESS. A DESTINATION OUT OF RANGE OF THE DETONATION SIGNAL. ONCE I KNOW THEY'RE IN THE CLEAR--
--I LET YOU GO.
REALLY, TERI?

AND AFTER YOUR BELOVED JUSTICE LEAGUE IS SAFE--
--HOW DO YOU GET OUT?
MAYBE I DON'T.

NOBLE SELF-SACRIFICE? HOW TRITE.
YOU NEVER COULD SEE THE WORLD BEYOND YOUR OWN SWOLLEN EGO, TERRY. HOW IS IT I NEVER UNDER-STOOD THAT--
--UNTIL NOW?
BLINDED BY SISTERLY LOVE, NO DOUBT.

NOT ANY MORE!

GIVE HER WHAT SHE WANTS.
WHAT?
I KNOW MY SISTER. I KNOW WHEN SHE'S BLUFFING...AND WHEN SHE'S SERIOUS.

"NOW GIVE HER WHAT SHE WANTS!"
...I DID IT! BOUGHT THE LEAGUE THE TIME THEY NEEDED! THEY'RE OFF WORLD! THEY'RE SAFE!
AS FOR ME? WELL, I GUESS I'LL JUST KEEP RUNNING...
...UNTIL THEY FINALLY STOP ME.
THAT WAS ONE HELL OF AN ACTING JOB I DID BACK THERE. HE MAY BE A MONSTER--BUT I COULD NEVER KILL MY BROTHER. FOR ALL HE'S DONE, I LOVE HIM TOO MUCH.
STILL--HE BELIEVED ME. GUESS WHEN A MURDERER LOOKS AT THE WORLD, ALL HE SEES IS BLOOD.
AND HE'S OUT FOR MINE NOW. THEY ALL ARE.
FUNNY THING IS--KNOWING THAT I'VE DIED ONCE ALREADY...
...I'M NOT AFRAID OF DYING AGAIN.
KEEP TRYING, CONVERT--
STONK
--MAYBE ONE OF THESE DAYS--
--YOU'LL ACTUALLY CATCH--
SMAK

MORTAL SCUM!
--ME...?!
YOU MAY ELUDE THESE OTHERS--
--BUT NOT THE GODDESS KALI!
BEING GENETICALLY ALTERED TO RESEMBLE AN ANCIENT DEITY DOESN'T ACTUALLY MAKE YOU ONE, KALI. BUT WE CAN DEBATE THEOLOGY LATER--
--AFTER THE SPEED BACKWASH.
"SPEED BACKWASH"? WHAT DO YOU--
DID YOU THINK THAT WOULD STOP ME?
HONESTLY? I WAS KIND OF HOPING IT WOULD.
FOOL! KALI IS THE GODDESS OF DEATH AND COSMIC DESTRUCTION! THE VERY EMBODIMENT OF--

KRONK
BORING... ISN'T SHE?
SUPERMAN!
GOD, I LOVE IT WHEN PEOPLE SAY MY NAME LIKE THAT! ALL THAT AWE AND WONDER GIVES ME GOOSE-BUMPS!
NOW, COME ON--
--WE'VE ONLY GOT A FEW SECONDS BEFORE THE TRANS-VERSAL BLOWS. AND THE LAST THING WE WANT TO DO--
--IS GET OURSELVES STUCK HERE WITH THESE JACKASSES.
YOU... YOU CAME BACK FOR ME.
OF COURSE! YOU THINK THE JUSTICE LEAGUE'S GONNA LEAVE ONE OF OUR OWN BEHIND?
ONE OF YOUR OWN? M-ME?
WELL, THINK OF YOURSELF AS A JUNIOR MEMBER.
YOU CAN GET ME COFFEE IN THE MORNING...KEEP TRACK OF THE WITTY THINGS I SAY...GIVE ME SUPER-SPEED MASSAGES--
YOU'RE JOKING, RIGHT?
YEAH, RIGHT, BABE-- THAT'S ME--
"--A LAUGH A MINUTE."
KROOM
ENJOY YOUR MOMENT OF GLORY, SISTER. BUT LET ME ASSURE YOU--
--IT WON'T LAST VERY LONG.

"TIME AND AGAIN WE'VE GIVEN
OU SAFE HARBOR, ARIEL MASTERS.
A PLACE TO HIDE FROM BOTH THE
IMPERIUM AND CADMUS."
"AND I'VE APPRECIATED THAT, YOUR HIGHNESS, BUT--"
"YET YOU BRING THESE OUTSIDERS HERE AND, WITH THEM, A NEW DANGER TO THE REALM."
"HEY! WE'RE NOT THE OUTSIDERS! WE'RE THE JUSTICE LEAGUE!"
"KEEP OUT OF THIS, SUPERMAN... PLEASE.
"YOUR HIGHNESS, IF YOU'LL JUST LET ME EXPLAIN: I HAD NO CHOICE BUT TO BRING THE LEAGUE TO CAMELOT NINE.
"WE HAD TO GET FAR ENOUGH FROM CADMUSWORLD SO THAT THE MICRO-MINES THAT WERE IMPLANTED IN THEM COULDN'T BE DETONATED BY--"
"NO MORE EXPLANATIONS!"

AFTER DECADES OF PEACE, WE ARE CAUGHT UP IN A DESPERATE WAR WITH ETRIGAN'S FORCES! ALL THAT WE KNOW...ALL THAT WE ARE... IS IN DANGER OF BEING CONSUMED BY THE DEMON'S DARK EMPIRE!
AND THEN YOU ARRIVE WITH THESE...COSTUMED INTERLOPERS-- AND THE FIVE ON YOUR TAIL!
JUSTICE LEAGUE 3000
THE CAMELOT WAR!

HAT WOULD OU HAVE ME DO?
THE RIGHT THING.
IT IS THE DECISION OF ARTHUR, KING OF THE NEW BRITONS, THAT YOU LEAVE THIS WORLD--
--NOW!
KEITH GIFFEN PLOT & BREAKDOWNS
J.M. DEMATTEIS SCRIPT
HOWARD PORTER ART
HI-FI COLORS · ROB LEIGH LETTERS
BRIAN CUNNINGHAM ONCE AND FUTURE KING
SIR HARVEY RICHARDS EDITOR

YOU DON'T UNDERSTAND, YOUR HIGHNESS--THE SITUATION ISN'T THE SAME AS BEFORE--
--TERRY AND THE FIVE HAVE ACCESS TO D.N.A. LABS THAT CONTAIN THE GENETIC BLUEPRINTS FOR EVERY METAHUMAN OF THE TWENTY-FIRST CENTURY!
IF WE DON'T STOP THEM, THEY'LL CREATE A SUPER-POWERED ARMY THAT COULD--
"WE"? YOU EXPECT ME TO JOIN IN YOUR WAR--WHEN CAMELOT IS ALREADY ENGAGED IN ANOTHER?
WAKE UP, ARTHUR! THIS WILL BE THE WAR TO END ALL WARS! AND IF YOU DON'T HELP--
YOU DARE ADDRESS A MONARCH IN SO DISRESPECTFUL A MANNER?
DAMN RIGHT I DO! WE'VE GOT TO--
WOULD YOU BOTH PLEASE SHUT UP?
ARE YOU CERTAIN THE FIVE WILL COME? CAMELOT HAS REMAINED BEYOND THEIR REACH SINCE THE COMMONWEALTH FELL.
NOT BEYOND THEIR REACH, GALAHAD--BEYOND THEIR INTEREST. THE FIVE WERE BUSY CONQUERING OTHER WORLDS.
THEY WOULD HAVE TURNED THEIR ATTENTIONS HERE EVENTUALLY.
AND YOUR COMING HAS NOW MADE THAT A CERTAINTY.
WHAT YOU CALL A CERTAINTY, I CALL-- A TRAP.
IF WE KNOW THEY'RE ON THEIR WAY, THEN WE CAN PREPARE FOR THEM.
ARIEL IS NOTHING IF NOT INGENIOUS, ARTHUR--AND, TIME AND AGAIN, SHE HAS PROVEN HERSELF WORTHY OF OUR TRUST.
WISE WORDS, MY LOVE LET ME MEDITATE UPO THIS.
YOU'DBETTER NOTTHINKTOO LONGORWE'RE ALLGONNABE WORMFOOD!
YOU'LL HAVE TO EXCUS THE FLASH, YOUR HIGHNESS SHE'S HAD A TERRIBLE SHOC RECENTLY--

"--AND IT'S LEFT HER MORE THAN A LITTLE... UNSTABLE."
UNSTABLE? HOW COULD YOU CALL ME THAT?
PLEASE, TERI--YOU WERE MURDERED BY YOUR TWIN BROTHER... THEN RESURRECTED WITH A MUTATED CELL STRUCTURE--
--COURTESY OF BARRY ALLEN'S D.N.A.
THAT WOULD MAKE ANYONE UNSTABLE!
I DON'T GO FOR THIS WHOLE KING BUSINESS: IT'S UN-AMERICAN!
SIGH WHATEVER YOU DO, CLARK--DON'T OFFEND THEM! ARTHUR AND GUINEVERE ARE JUST AND COMPASSIONATE RULERS AND--
AND WHAT DOES THAT MATTER WITH TERRY ON THE WAY?
MAYBE YOU'VE USED THIS WORLD AS A HIDING PLACE TILL NOW, BUT--
YOU'RE AFRAID--AREN'T YOU?
OF COURSE I'M AFRAID! I'M NOT LIKE YOU! I'M NO HERO!
YOU CERTAINLY ACTED LIKE ONE BACK ON CADMUS WORLD. WITHOUT YOU, KID--WE NEVER WOULD HAVE GOTTEN OUT.
DUMB LUCK!
OR BARRY'S D.N.A.--URGING YOU ON TO ACTIONS YOU WOULD OTHERWISE BE INCAPABLE OF.
HEY--IF THIS PLACE IS LIKE THE KING ARTHUR STORIES I READ AS A KID--
IT IS AND IT ISN'T.
--THEN AREN'T THERE WIZARDS HERE? AND COULDN'T THEY JUST...Y'KNOW...PUT A WHAMMY ON THE FIVE?
YOU HEARD WHAT ARTHUR SAID--HE'S AT WAR WITH AN ARMY OF DEMONS. ALL HIS MAGICIANS ARE OTHERWISE ENGAGED.
IS THAT WHY YOU'RE MAKING ADJUSTMENTS TO CAMELOT NINE'S TRANSVERSAL SYSTEM?

EXACTLY. THE FIVE WILL BE USING A GATE TO MAKE LANDFALL AND...WITH ARTHUR'S PERMISSION... I JUST EMBEDDED A VIRUS THAT WILL--
WELL, LET'S JUST SAY IT'LL GIVE THEM A WELCOME THEY WON'T FORGET.
AND YOU THINK THIS WILL STOP THEM?
OF COURSE NOT. BUT IT SHOULD THROW OFF THEIR GAME LONG ENOUGH FOR YOU FIVE TO TAKE THEM DOWN.
YOU MAKE IT SOUND SO EASY.
I DON'T MEAN TO, BATMAN. I'M JUST TRYING TO GIVE US A FIGHTING CHANCE.
AND WE'RE GOING TO NEED IT. AFTER THE DEFEAT WE JUST HANDED THEM, TERRY'S GOING TO BE FROTHING AT THE MOUTH. ONE THING I KNOW ABOUT MY BROTHER--
HE'S A VERY BAD LOSER.
WE'VE FACED WORSE THAN THIS IN THE PAST, FLASH--AND WE'VE ALWAYS--
WHY THE HELL ARE YOU CALLING HER "FLASH"? THE FLASH WAS A MAN NAMED BARRY ALLEN--
--AND WE HAVEN'T EVEN HAD A CHANCE TO MOURN HIM.
THIS ISN'T THE TIME FOR MOURNING, HAL. THIS IS THE TIME TO STOP TERRY ONCE AND FOR ALL.
SO YOU'VE GOT A PLAN?
CAMELOT NINE WAS BUILT UPON THE UNDERGROUND RUINS OF AN ANCIENT CIVILIZATION. I SAY WE LURE THE FIVE DOWN INTO THOSE RUINS--

"--AND MAKE OUR FINAL STAND THERE."
ADMUSWORLD...
...I WANT HER DEAD!
I WANT THEM ALL DEAD!
SO YOU KEEP SAYING.
YOU WANT 'EM DEAD? FINE. I'LL TURN THEM ALL INTO GOLDFISH AND FLUSH THEM DOWN THE NEAREST TOILET.
NOT GOOD ENOUGH, LOCUS!
I WANT THEM TO SUFFER. I WANT THEM TO EXPERIENCE AGONIES THAT NO HUMAN BEING HAS EVER KNOWN BEFORE! I WANT THEM TO--
LISTEN TO ME, TERRY: THIS KIND OF OVEREMOTIONAL RESPONSE IS JUST WHAT ARIEL EXPECTS.
SHE WANTS US TO COME BLUNDERING AFTER THEM WITH NO PLAN, NO--
YOU LISTEN TO ME, COEVAL: I'VE BEEN PLANNING AND PLOTTING... MANIPULATING AND SCHEMING...ALL MY LIFE!
WHAT I WANT NOW IS ACTION! WHAT I WANT NOW--

"--IS BLOOD!"
...EVEN IN RUINS, THIS PLACE IS MAGNIFICENT. WHAT WAS IT--BEFORE IT FELL?
HOME TO SOME LONG-FORGOTTEN RACE, I ASSUME. NO ON KNOWS FOR SURE. A LO OF HISTORY WAS LOST AFTER THE GREAT DISASTER.
CAN YOU FEEL IT? THERE'S AN ENERGY HERE... A POWER... THAT'S--
WELL, IT'S... HUMBLING.
"HUMBLING"? NOW THERE'S A WORD I NEVER EXPECTED TO COME OUT OF SUPEREGO'S MOUTH.
DON'T START.
HOW'RE THINGS GOING WITH THE 'VERSAL?
NO ACTIVITY YET.
THEY'LL BE HERE SOON ENOUGH.
YOUR FEAR WILL BE THE DEATH OF YOU, TERI.
NO, MY BROTHER WILL BE THE DEATH OF ME.
TAKE HEART, GIRL: I'VE LEARNED, FIRSTHAND, THAT THE THOUGHT OF DYIN IS FAR WORSE THAN THE ACTUAL EXPERIENCE.
SOMEHOW--

--I DON'T FIND THAT VERY COMFORTING.
WHAT IS IT WE'RE WAITING FOR EXACTLY?
ONCE TERRY ENTERS CAMELOT'S COORDINATES INTO THE CADMUS SYSTEM WE'LL GET AN ALERT HERE--
AND...?
AND HE'S GOING TO BE IN FOR AN EXTREMELY UNPLEASANT--
"--SURPRISE."
COORDINATES LOCKED, COEVAL?
LOCKED.
EXCELLENT. ONCE WE'RE THROUGH--KILL EVERYONE IN SIGHT.
"BUT LEAVE TERI FOR ME."
...SO YOU'RE SAYING THAT ALL THE TRANSVERSALS ACROSS THE GALAXY SHARE A COMMON FREQUENCY?
IT'S THE ONLY WAY FOR THEM TO FUNCTION WITHOUT--
--HANG ON!
"THEY'VE ACTIVATED!"
WHERE'S COEVAL?
DOWNLOADED INTO MY BIO-IMPLANTS FOR THE JOURNEY.
HOW--
RUMMMMMMMM
RUMMMMMMMMMMMMMMMM
--ROMANTIC.
WAIT A MINUTE! THIS CAN'T BE RIGHT!
DAMMIT! THE BITCH HACKED THE SYSTEM!

IT'S A TRAP!
Y'THINK?
M'LORD ETRIGAN--
--THE CASTLE HAS BEEN BREACHED!
WHAT BRINGS THEM HERE BEFORE MY THRONE? SUCH FOOLISHNESS HAS NE'ER BEEN KNOWN!
ETRIGAN'S ORDER, ETRIGAN'S WHIM: TEAR THEM BLOODY LIMB FROM LIMB!
"ONCE THE FIVE REALIZE WHAT THEY'RE UP AGAINST--"

--WON'T THEY JUST 'PORT OUT OF THERE?
THEY'LL TRY. BUT ETRIGAN AND HIS ARMY WON'T LET THEM GO WITHOUT A FIGHT.
AND I CAN ASSURE YOU THAT IT WILL BE A VERY NASTY ONE. AND WITH A LITTLE LUCK, THEY'LL--
YOUR LUCK HAS FINALLY RUN OUT, MASTERS.
FIRST WE'RE GOING TO TAKE YOU AND YOUR PRECIOUS HEROES--
RUMMMMMMMM
--AND THEN WE'RE TAKING THIS WORLD.
CLEVER TRICK, ARIEL. THOSE DEMONS WERE A FORMIDABLE LOT. BUT WE'RE THE FIVE--
--AND WE'RE INVINCIBLE.
HERE'S THE THING ABOUT OVERCONFIDENCE, TERRY: IT MAKES YOU SLOPPY. AND THAT--

--CAN BE DANGEROUS.
BA-WOOOOM
FOOLS! DID YOU ACTUALLY THINK DETONATING THE GATE WOULD STOP US?
NO, KALI. BUT YOU HAVE TO ADMIT IT DID A GOOD JOB OF TRAPPING YOU HERE IN THESE RUINS WHERE YOU CAN DO THE LEAST DAMAGE!
ALL YOU'VE DONE IS DESTROY YOUR ONLY AVENUE OF RETREAT!
WE NEVER RETREAT! WE NEVER SURRENDER!
AND DO YOU KNOW WHY?

BECAUSE WE'RE THE JUSTICE LEAGUE
--AND WHATEVER THE CENTURY... WHATEVER THE THREAT--
--WE ALWAYS PREVAIL!

WHAT DID SHE JUST SAY?!
NO HORDES OF INNOCENTS DOWN HERE FOR YOU TO POSSESS, CONVERT--
--NO MIND-CONTROLLED ARMIES TO HIDE BEHIND--
--SO LET'S SEE HOW YOU DO ONE-ON-ONE!
I COULD POSSESS YOU, BAT--
--BUT THAT WOULD ROB ME OF THE PLEASURE OF BEATING YOU TO A BLOODY PUL--
WOMP
KRAAAK
WHAP
STONNK

CHIKKA CHIKKA CHIKKA
YOU WERE SAYING...?
YOU WON'T BE... SO SMUG--
--WHEN I... INSERT MY CONSCIOUSNESS... INTO YOURS AND--
BACK IN THE 21ST CENTURY WE CALLED THAT MACE.
STINGS LIKE A SONUVABITCH--
PSSSSH
ARRR--!
--DOESN'T IT?
HOW DID YOU DO IT, JORDAN?
HOW DID YOU RETURN TO NORMAL--AFTER I REDUCED YOU TO THE SIZE OF A FRIGHTENED LITTLE MOUSE?
NEVER UNDERESTIMATE THE GREEN ENERGY, LOCUS: A LITTLE WILLPOWER AND I CAN DO JUST ABOUT ANYTHING!
ANYTHING--
--EXCEPT TOPPLE A GOD!
AND THIS GOD IS GOING TO SHRINK YOU AND SHRINK YOU TILL A MICROBE SEEMS LIKE A PLANET! TILL A PROTON SEEMS LIKE A UNIVER--
WHAT THE HELL--?

WHY ARE YOU STILL THERE?
I'M A GOD! I'M A GOD AND I SHRUNK YOU AND--
AND YOU NEVER LEARN... DO YOU?
WAIT. HOW...HOW CAN YOU BE THERE WHEN YOU'RE--?
BECAUSE THE GUY IN THE CLOAK IS A CONSTRUCT.
WELL, MORE LIKE A FULLY MANIFESTED EXTENSION OF MY MIND. I THINK--
MMPHH!
--AND IT OBEYS!
'COURSE MY MIND ISN'T HALF AS POWERFUL AS YOURS--
--BUT IT'S HARD TO USE ALL THAT POWER, ISN'T IT--
WOMMP
--WHEN YOU'RE UNCONSCIOUS?
HANG ON, DIANA--

SKRAKOOM
--I'VE GOT YOUR BACK!
YOU LAY ONE FINGER ON MY BACK AND I'LL--
I'M NOT TRYING TO COP A FEEL-- I'M TRYING TO HELP YOU!
WHAT YOU SAID BACK THERE: "NO MATTER THE CENTURY, NO MATTER THE THREAT..." YOU WERE RIGHT. WE'RE A HELLUVA TEAM AND--
TAKA-TOOM
GET THIS STRAIGHT, KENT--
--I DON'T NEED YOUR HELP!
FINE! BE THAT WAY!
HEY-- WHERE DO YOU THINK YOU'RE GOING?
BUT YOU JUST SAID--
THAT I DIDN'T NEED YOUR HELP--
--NOT THAT I DIDN'T WANT IT!
ALL RIGHT! I KNEW THAT DEEP DOWN YOU STILL HAD THE HOTS FOR ME!
Sigh STUFF YOUR LIBIDO BACK IN YOUR SHORTS, WILL YOU--

--AND LET'S KICK KALI'S ASS!
FOOLS! I WILL SUCK THE SOULS OUT OF YOUR BODIES! ADD YOUR VERY LIFE-FORCE TO MY OWN AND--
DO US ALL A FAVOR, KALI--
AND
SHUT
THE
KROMMM
UP!
Y'KNOW, CLARK--YOU MAY BE AN ARROGANT IMBECILE WITH DELUSIONS OF GRANDEUR--
--BUT YOU'RE A GOOD MAN TO HAVE AROUND IN A FIGHT.
A BACKHANDED COMPLIMENT?
WE'RE REALLY MAKING PROGRESS-- AREN'T WE, GORGEOUS?
GET UP, DAMN YOU--

--AND FIGHT!
I KNOW YOU, SIS: I DON'T PUT UP A STRUGGLE, YOU WON'T LAY A HAND ON ME.
YOU'VE STILL GOT THE BRUISES FROM THE LAST TIME I DIDN'T LAY A HAND ON YOU.
EVEN I CAN SEE THAT YOU STILL LOVE TERRY. WHY NOT JOIN US? USE YOUR NEWFOUND POWER IN SERVICE TO THE FIVE?
COEVAL'S RIGHT. THE LEAGUE DOESN'T STAND A CHANCE AGAINST US. LOCUS ALONE HAS THE POWER TO WIPE YOU ALL OUT OF EXISTENCE.
I'D LOVE TO HAVE YOU BY MY SIDE AGAIN.
SAID THE MAN WHO MURDERED ME.
MAYBE...I MADE A MISTAKE. OR MAYBE I KNEW EXACTLY WHAT ARIEL WOULD DO IF I KILLED YOU.
MAYBE I WANTED YOU TO BECOME THE FLASH.
OR MAYBE YOU'RE JUST A COWARD AND A LIAR.
IN ANY CASE, YOU'RE RIGHT ABOUT ONE THING: I COULD NEVER REALLY HURT YOU. NO MATTER WHAT YOU'VE DONE, YOU'RE STILL MY BROTHER.
WHICH IS WHY I HAD NO CHOICE BUT TO KEEP YOU DISTRACTED AND TALKING--
--UNTIL SHE WAS READY FOR YOU.
SHE...?
ME.
G-GET BACK OR I'LL--
YOU'LL WHAT? DETONATE THE MICRO-MINES?
TRANSVERSAL'S BLOWN. YOU CAN'T USE IT TO GET OUT-- WHICH MEANS THAT IF WE GO UP--
--YOU'RE CAUGHT IN THE BLAST.
COEVAL! COEVAL-- HELP ME!
COEVAL...?

DON'T LEAVE ME...!
YOU THINK COEVAL'S REALLY GONE?
NO PLACE FOR HIM TO UPLOAD IN THE RUINS. NONE OF US HAVE ANY IMPLANTS TO HIDE AWAY IN. THE GATE'S COLLAPSED.
HE'S STILL IN THERE...LYING LOW, CALCULATING--
--BUT HE CAN'T BE VERY COMFORTABLE RIGHT NOW.
DON'T BREAK HIM!
Y'KNOW, YOU WERE ALL PRETTY DAMN MAGNIFICENT TODAY.
THE JUSTICE LEAGUE IS EVERYTHING I IMAGINED IT TO BE... AND SO MUCH MORE.
WE GOT LUCKY-- THAT'S ALL.
OH, STOP WITH ALL THE DOWNBEAT "CREATURE OF THE NIGHT" CRAP. THE LEAGUE TOOK ON THE BIGGEST, BADDEST BASTARDS IN THE UNIVERSE TODAY AND WE WON--
--THE WAY WE ALWAYS DO.
"ALWAYS," huh? HAVE YOU CONVENIENTLY FORGOTTEN OUR FINAL BATTLE WHEN WE WERE ALL SLAUGHTERED BY--
I DON'T WANNA TALK ABOUT THAT!
GEEZ! YOU ARE SUCH A BUMMER.
YOU KNOW WHAT YOU FIVE NEED NOW?
A SHOWER, A BOTTLE OF SCOTCH AND A GOOD NIGHT'S SLEEP?
NO: A HEADQUARTERS.
A WHAT?
THAT'S A GREAT IDEA!
NO, IT'S NOT!

CADMUSWORLD...
...ON A VERY GRIM DAY...
JUSTICE LEAGUE 3000
A NEW BEGINNING
WELCOME HOME, SIR.
GIVEN YOUR RATHER BELLICOSE TONE--
WHO ASKED YOU?
--AND THE FACT THAT LOCUS AND KALI AREN'T WITH YOU--
--I CAN ONLY ASSUME THAT THINGS DIDN'T GO AS PLANNED ON CAMELOT NINE.
TO SAY THE LEAST.
KEITH GIFFEN, J.M. DEMATTEIS, HOWARD PORTER, HI-FI, TAYLOR ESPOSITO, HARVEY RICHARDS and BRIAN CUNNINGHAM are warning you:
DON'T LOOK AT THE LAST PAGE UNTIL YOU REACH THE END OF THE STORY!*
*ADMIT IT: YOU LOOKED, DIDN'T YOU? WE KNEW YOU WOULD.

I CAN BECOME AN ARMY OF A MILLION... A BILLION...AND I PROMISE YOU, TERRY--
--THE JUSTICE LEAGUE WILL PAY FOR THIS IGNOMINIOUS DEFEAT AND--
SPARE ME THE HISTRIONICS, CONVERT.
IF YOU COULD HAVE STOPPED THEM, YOU WOULD HAVE--WHEN IT COUNTED. BUT YOU FAILED...YOU ALL DID!
AND SO DID I.
OFF TO YOUR QUARTERS TO SULK, SIR?
OFF TO MY QUARTERS TO PLAN.
...THIS LOOKS SUSPICIOUSLY LIKE SULKING TO ME.
SHUT UP-- WILL YOU, RONALD?
I'VE SERVED YOUR FAMILY FOR FOUR GENERATIONS, SIR. I FEEL THAT IT'S MY JOB TO--
TO ANNOY ME?
TO LOOK AFTER YOU. YOU AND YOUR SISTER.
MY SISTER? SHE'S DEAD. OR AT LEAST SHE SHOULD BE.
SIGH BUT SOME-HOW SHE CAME BACK...WITH THE FLASH'S POWERS--
--AND SHE HUMILIATED ME!
SHE LET YOU GO, SIR. THAT SEEMS EXTRAORDINARILY GENEROUS OF TERI--
--CONSIDERING YOU MURDERED HER.
IT WASN'T TERI WHO MADE THE DEAL, RONALD. IT WAS THAT WITCH--

"--ARIEL MASTERS..."
CAMELOT NINE.
FORTY-EIGHT HOURS EARLIER...
SO HERE'S HOW IT PLAYS OUT, TERRY.
YOU REMOVE THE MICRO-MINES YOU IMPLANTED IN THE JUSTICE LEAGUE AND--
AND I JUST WALK OUT OF HERE?
WHY DON'T I BELIEVE YOU?
BECAUSE YOU'RE INCAPABLE OF UNDERSTANDING SIMPLE HUMAN COMPASSION.
YOU--HAVE COMPASSION FOR ME?
NO. BUT YOUR SISTER DOES. GOD ONLY KNOWS WHY.
ME...I'M A PRAGMATIST. YOU DESIGNED AND IMPLANTED THOSE MINES--KEYED TO YOUR OWN BIOLOGICAL IMPRINT.
I TRY TO NEUTRALIZE THEM AND THEY'LL DETONATE. YOU'RE THE ONLY ONE WHO CAN DO IT.
AND IF I DON'T...?
YOU ROT HERE IN PERMANENT STASIS--ALONG WITH THE REST OF THE FIVE.
YOU DON'T HAVE ALL OF THEM, ARIEL. THE CONVERT IS STILL OUT THERE AND--
THEN YOUR ANSWER IS NO?

YOU SAY MY SISTER HAS COMPASSION FOR ME?
I SAY IT'S HUBRIS. TERI HAS ME WHERE SHE WANTS ME--
--WHERE'S SHE'S ALWAYS WANTED ME: AT HER MERCY.
SHE'S JEALOUS OF ME...RESENTS ALL THE YEARS STANDING IN MY SHADOW--
--AND NOW SHE GETS TO LORD IT OVER ME. WELL, WE'LL SEE HOW LONG THAT LASTS!
YOU DON'T GET IT, DO YOU? THIS IS YOUR ONLY CHANCE-- AND YOU JUST BLEW IT.
GUARDS! COME AND TAKE THIS WEASEL TO THE--
NO. NO!
I'LL DO IT!
I'LL DO IT.
"AND I'M GLAD YOU DID, SIR. NOW YOU CAN PUT THIS BEHIND YOU AND--"
BEHIND ME? NO.
I KILLED TERI ONCE... AND I SWEAR TO GOD--

"--I'LL DO IT AGAIN."
CAMELOT NINE. now.
ARE YOU SURE THAT WILL HOLD THEM, LANCELOT? LOOKS DAMN FLIMSY.
LOOKS CAN BE DECEIVING, M'LADY DIANA.
"M'LADY"? HER?
DO YOU SEE THOSE RUNES CARVED IN THE ARCHWAY? THEIR ARCANE POWER WILL KEEP LOCUS, KALI AND CONVERT TRAPPED IN THERE TILL TIME'S END--AND BEYOND.
FIRST OF ALL-- YOU'VE ONLY GOT ONE CONVERT. THERE'S A ZILLION MORE RUNNING AROUND OUT THERE. SECOND OF ALL--
--RUNES? REALLY? YOU THINK YOU'RE GONNA STOP THEM WITH HOCUS-POCUS?
THAT "HOCUS POCUS" WAS USED TO RESTRAIN ETRIGAN'S HOSTS. NO WARRIOR... NO MAGICIAN...NO DEMON FROM THE PITS OF HELL...CAN BREAK THOSE MYSTIC SEALS.
UH-HUH. AND WHERE, MAY I ASK, IS COEVAL?
BONDED INTO THE RUNES THEM-SELVES.
OF COURSE HE IS.

DON'T MOCK WHAT YOU DON'T UNDERSTAND, SUPERMAN.
WHY NOT?
THAT SAID...I TRUST MAGIC EVEN LESS THAN I TRUST THE FIVE--
--SO LET'S KILL THE DOGS AND BE DONE WITH IT.
VIOLENCE? IS THAT YOUR ANSWER TO EVERYTHING?
YES.
I WILL TAKE MY LEAVE NOW. THAT IS--
--UNLESS YOU HAVE ANY MORE DIRE THREATS TO UNLEASH UPON MY WORLD.
WE'RE TRULY SORRY FOR THE TROUBLE WE'VE BROUGHT YOU--BUT THE FIVE HAD TO BE STOPPED AND--
AND WE'RE SO VERY GRATEFUL YOU CHOSE TO STOP THEM HERE.
GOOD DAY TO YOU ALL.
'BYE, LANCE.
DID SHE JUST CALL HIM "LANCE"?
ONE FINAL WORD BEFORE I DEPART--
--DO NOT TOUCH THE OTHER CONTAINMENT MOUNDS.
PRETTY ARROGANT FOR A GUY WHO RIDES A LITTLE TIN HORSEY.
AND WHEN IT COMES TO ARROGANCE--YOU'RE THE EXPERT.
HAR-HAR. ALL OF A SUDDEN YOU'RE A BAT-COMEDIAN.
C'MON, LET'S FIND ARIEL AND PUT SOME DISTANCE BETWEEN US AND THESE ARMORED JACKASSES.
YOU CAN SAY WHAT YOU WANT ABOUT ARTHUR AND HIS KNIGHTS...BUT YOU HAVE TO ADMIT--

--THEY'VE GOT ONE HELL OF A PRISON SYSTEM.
"THE JUSTICE LEAGUE SAMPLES ARE WHAT?"

"CORRUPTED. USELESS."
"HOW? NO... DON'T TELL ME."
ARIEL.
SHE MUST HAVE DONE IT WHILE SHE HAD ACCESS TO THE D.N.A. VAULT.
ACCESS, I HASTEN TO ADD, THAT YOU GAVE HER.
IT WAS COEVAL'S JOB TO MONITOR HER, NOT MINE!
SIGH
THERE'S ENOUGH BLAME FOR ALL OF US TO SHARE. AND LET'S FACE IT--
--ARIEL MASTERS IS AS DUPLICITOUS AS SHE IS BRILLIANT.
DAMN IT! I WANTED A JUSTICE LEAGUE TO DEFEAT THE JUSTICE LEAGUE!
HOW MANY OTHER SAMPLES WERE CORRUPTED?
JUST THOSE. MORE THAN THAT AND ARIEL WOULD HAVE RISKED DISCOVERY.
THEN WE STILL HAVE THE UPPER HAND, DON'T WE?
WE DO?
LET'S TAKE A STROLL DOWN TO THE VAULT--SHALL WE, CONVERT? HAVE A LOOK AROUND. SEE WHAT RAW MATERIAL IS AVAILABLE TO US.
I THINK IT'S TIME I CREATED--

"--A LEAGUE OF MY *OWN*."
...*THERE* YOU ARE.
SIGH NEVER A MOMENT'S *PEACE*.
WHAT'S THE CRISIS *NOW?*
NO CRISIS. I WAS JUST... *WANDERING* AND--
AND HOW *LUCKY* I AM THAT YOU *FOUND* ME.
I-I'M *SORRY*, ARIEL. I DIDN'T MEAN TO *INTERRUPT*. I'LL LEAVE YOU AL--
I WASN'T BEING SARCASTIC, *BRUCE*. I'M HAPPY TO *SEE* YOU.
YOU *SURE?*

YEAH. GUESS IT'S NOT JUST THE LEAGUE FACING AN UNCERTAIN FUTURE. YOU BURNED ALL YOUR BRIDGES WHEN YOU LEFT THE PROJECT--
CADMUS WAS THE ONLY LIFE I'VE EVER KNOWN. BUT I GUESS IT'S TIME TO CARVE OUT A NEW ONE.
HERE ON CAMELOT?
SEEMS LIKE THE PERFECT PLACE FOR US TO SET UP SHOP.
"US"?
I'VE ALREADY GOT ARTHUR'S PERMISSION. NOW ALL WE NEED TO DO IS FIX IT UP A LITTLE AND--
YOU'RE JOKING, RIGHT?
ACCORDING TO WHAT I'VE READ, YOU USED TO OPERATE OUT OF A CAVE.
DON'T YOU THINK THIS IS A STEP UP?
WELL, IF THIS IS GOING TO BE JUSTICE LEAGUE HEAD-QUARTERS--

ME GO! PLEASE!
I...I'VE CHANGED MY MIND!
A PROBLEM?
HAVING SECOND THOUGHTS.
REALLY? WHY?
I'VE...I'VE HEARD THE RUMORS...ABOUT WHAT YOU DO HERE! IF I'D KNOWN I NEVER WOULD HAVE SIGNED THOSE PAPERS! I--
AND WOULD YOU HAVE ACCEPTED THAT RATHER GENEROUS PAYMENT?

CURED YOUR SON OF IMSKIAN FEVER?
OR THE BEAUTIFUL NEW HOME WE PROVIDED?
I'LL GIVE IT ALL BACK! I'LL...I'LL PAY FOR THE VACCINE!
BELIEVE ME, DEAR-- YOU COULDN'T AFFORD IT.

I'M NOT WITHOUT A HEART. I'D BE HAPPY TO RELEASE YOU FROM YOUR CONTRACT--
YOU WOULD?
--BUT, UNFORTUNATELY, YOUR GENETIC STRUCTURE IS CLOSEST TO WHAT WE NEED--

--SO IT'S OFF TO THE LAB WITH YOU!
BUT MY HUSBAND! MY CHILDREN!
DON'T CONCERN YOURSELF ABOUT THEM. ONCE WE'VE HAD OUR WAY WITH YOU--
--YOU WON'T REMEMBER THEY EVER EXISTED.
NOOOOOOO--!
THEY ALWAYS GET SO AGITATED WHEN THEY DISCOVER WHAT WE'RE REALLY DOING HERE. IT'S ACTUALLY

"WHICH IS WHY I ALWAYS MAKE SURE THEY FIND OUT."
HELLO...?
MR. KENT...?
NOW WHERE DID HE--
NOT... HUFF... KENT!
SUPER... HUFF... MAN!
HEY... ARE YOU OKAY?
ME? I'M... PUFF... FINE. NEVER... PUFF... BETTER.
I MEAN... HUFF... FOR CRYIN' OUT LOUD... PUFF... I'M THE GREATEST SUPERHERO WHO EVER...

SUPERMAN...?
HUFF
PUFF
HUFFA-PUFFA-HUFFA
HUFF
HAKK
HUFFATA-PUFFATA
GASP
ANOTHER RACE?
AT LEAST HE DIDN'T THROW UP THIS TIME.
WHEN'S HE GOING TO ADMIT THAT YOU CAN BEAT HIM?
I THINK HE'S JUST PRETENDING. Y'KNOW...TO BOLSTER MY CONFIDENCE.
SURE. JUST LIKE HE PRETENDS TO BE A NARCISSISTIC ASS.
THAT'S NOT VERY NICE, HAL.
YOU CAN'T GET CONFIDENCE FROM HIM--YOU'VE GOT TO FIND IT IN YOURSELF. YOU'RE THE FLASH NOW, TERI. THAT NAME MEANS SOMETHING.
BARRY ALLEN... HE WAS--HE WAS THE BEST. NOT JUST AS A COSTUMED HERO-- BUT AS A HUMAN BEING. THAT'S A LOT TO LIVE UP TO.
DON'T LET ME DOWN.
AND CLARK...?
HUFF... PUFF... HUFFA-PUFFA...?
SHE'S FASTER THAN YOU.

"GET OVER IT."
...SO TELL ME, CONVERT--
--WHAT DOES YOUR REAL BODY LOOK LIKE?
A GIRL'S GOT TO HAVE HER SECRETS.
GIRL?
FOR TODAY, ANYWAY.
SPEAKING OF SECRETS--HAVE THEY BEEN BRIEFED?
I THINK YOU'RE MAKING A MISTAKE HERE, TERRY. ACCELERATING THE PROCESS IS BEYOND DANGEROUS AND--
HAVE THEY BEEN BRIEFED?
AS ORDERED, YES, BUT--
YOUR OBJECTIONS HAVE BEEN NOTED. NOW WHAT ARE YOUR IMPRESSIONS OF THEM?
UNTRUSTWORTHY. UNPREDICTABLE. UNSTABLE.
UNLIKE LOCUS OR KALI--WHO WERE THE EPITOME OF SANITY AND DEPENDABILITY.
AND PERHAPS THAT'S WHY THE LEAGUE DEFEATED US.
THE LEAGUE DEFEATED US BECAUSE WE DIDN'T REALLY UNDERSTAND THEM. THEY WERE JUST... VAGUE LEGENDS TO US.
WE NEED SOLDIERS WHO KNOW SUPERMAN AND THE OTHERS INTIMATELY--
--AND HATE THEM WITH A PASSION THAT TIME CAN'T DIM.
WHO THE HELL ARE YOU?

I RAISED YOU UP FROM YOUR GRAVES--
--AND BREATHED NEW LIFE INTO YOUR MOLDERING CORPSES.
WELL... GOD--Y'DID A LOUSY JOB. FEELS LIKE THERE ARE ELEPHANT-SIZED HOLES IN MY MEMORY.
IT'S TRUE THAT YOUR MEMORIES MAY BE SLIGHTLY IMPAIRED--BUT I'VE COMPENSATED FOR THAT LACK BY ENHANCING YOUR POWERS. UPGRADING YOUR D.N.A.
AND I TRUST YOU REMEMBER THE IMPORTANT THINGS--
--LIKE BREAKING BATMAN'S BACK?
LIKE IT WAS YESTERDAY.
THEN WELCOME TO THE INJUSTICE LEAGUE, BANE.
AND YOU... CAPTAIN COLD--
THE NAME'S MIRROR MASTER.
MIRROR MASTER. CAPTAIN COLD. HOW AM I SUPPOSED TO KEEP TRACK OF THESE INANE NAMES?
HOW DARE YOU--?
OFFENDED? DON'T BE. ONCE YOU SEE HOW I'VE AUGMENTED YOUR ABILITIES--
--YOU'LL BE KISSING MY RING.
SPEAKING OF WHICH-- WHERE THE DEVIL IS MY RING?
YOU'RE AS BAD AS JORDAN. WHINE, WHINE, WHINE.
YOU DON'T NEED YOUR PRECIOUS JEWELRY ANY-MORE, SINESTRO. YOU ARE THE RING.
AND ME? WHAT COULD A HUMAN WHELP LIKE YOU POSSIBLY DO TO IMPROVE UPON ZEUS--LORD OF OLYMPUS?
FOR STARTERS, I MIXED IN THE GENETIC MATERIAL OF SEVERAL OTHER GODHEADS--SO YOU'RE TWICE THE DEITY YOU USED TO BE.
AND, FINALLY...THE LEGENDARY LOIS LANE! WHEN THOSE D.N.A. SPLICES KICK IN--AS THEY SHOULD BE DOING ANY MOMENT--
--YOU'LL BE ON YOUR KNEES BEGGING ME TO MARRY YOU!
SORRY, KID. YOU'RE TOO YOUNG FOR ME.

OH, COME ON, LOIS: WHAT'S A THOUSAND YEARS BETWEEN FRIENDS?
CUT T'THE CHASE. WHY'D YOU BRING US BACK? WHADDAYOU WANT FROM US?
I WANT YOU TO DO WHAT YOU'VE ALWAYS DREAMED OF DOING: KILL THE JUSTICE LEAGUE.
ALL EXCEPT FOR THE FLASH: SHE'S MINE.
WAIT A MINUTE! "SHE"--?
LONG STORY.
AND IF WE DO WHAT YOU'RE ASKING--WHAT DO WE GET IN RETURN?
SATISFACTION FOR ONE THING... AND A WHOLE NEW UNIVERSE--
--RIPE FOR THE TAKING!
AND IF WE DECLINE...?
GET REAL, POPS. NOBODY HERE'S TURNING DOWN THIS OFFER.

GET THIS PARTY STARTED."
THE PRISON PLANET TAKRON-GALTOS...
...FORMERLY KNOWN AS--EARTH.
GEEZ! I CAN'T BELIEVE WE'RE BUILDING ANOTHER APARTMENT BLOCK! I MEAN, HOW MANY CRIMINALS CAN THEY SHIP T'THIS CRUMMY PLACE?
THAT AIN'T OUR PROBLEM, HERB.
YER RIGHT, ERNESTO. OUR PROBLEM'S MAKIN' SURE THE DAMN SEA WALL'S BULKED UP.

YEAH. WE'RE GOIN' PRETTY DEEP--AN' IF WE GET SEEPAGE FROM ALL THAT TOXIC GUNK DOWN THERE--
--THIS WHOLE PROJECT COULD BE SCRAPPED.
WHICH ANS YOU 'N' ME BE OUT OF A ...AND PROB'LY OUR ASSES PPED OUT T'THE WASTES.
THAT WOULDN'T BE TOO GOOD, HERB. THOSE LUNATICS OUT IN THE WASTES GET THEIR HANDS ON US, THEY'LL--
HEY, YOU GUYS!
WHAT'RE YOU YELLIN' ABOUT, GROVE?
EXCAVATION CREW FOUND SOMETHING!
NOT ANOTHER FREAKIN' SUBWAY TUNNEL...?
NAH. SOME KINDA CHAMBER OR SOMETHIN'. BIRDIE THINKS IT MIGHT BE CRYOGENIC!
CRYOGENIC? COME ON--NO ONE DOES THE DEEP FREEZE ANYMORE!
YEAH--WELL, THIS CHAMBER'S PLENTY OLD. SO OLD THAT BIRDIE'S CHRONOP COULDN'T EVEN DATE IT!
PLEASE! BIRDIE'S BEEN HUFFIN' FUMES DOWN THERE FOR SO LONG, SHE DOESN'T EVEN KNOW HOW OLD HER OWN MOTHER IS!
YEAH? WELL, COME SEE FOR YOURSELF!
OH I'M COMIN' ALL RIGHT!
KEEP AN EYE ON THINGS UP HERE, ERNESTO.
DON'T I

CRAP! IT IS CRYOGENIC! HOW MANY CANISTERS, BIRDIE?
TWO.
ANY IDENTIFYING MARKERS?
NO. THEY'VE GOT OLD-FASHIONED DATA CHIPS THAT BURNED OUT A LONG TIME AGO.
THEN WE BETTER OPEN THOSE SUCKERS UP!
YOU SURE ABOUT THIS, BOSS? WHAT IF THERE'S...I DUNNO...SOMETHIN' DANGEROUS INSIDE?
WE'RE ON A PLANET WITH EIGHT MILLION CONVICTS! WHAT'S MORE DANGEROUS THAN THAT? NOW, C'MON--WE GOT US A SCHEDULE T'KEEP--
--SO OPEN 'EM UP!
OKAY--BUT ANY-THING GOES WRONG--
KLAK
RAAK
--IT'S ON YOUR HEAD!
I GOT ONE QUESTION--
YEAH...?
PSSHHH

WHO THE HELL ARE THEY?

..hrrmmm...
sHNort
sHNort
OH, MAN... ≷yawwwn≶...THAT WAS ONE WEIRD DREAM.
ME 'N' BOOSTER IN SUSPENDED ANIMATION FOR A THOUSAND YEARS--
--WAKING UP IN SOME FREAKY FUTURE.
THAT YOU, TED?
IT WAS LAST TIME I LOOKED.
LOOK--WE'VE GOTTA TALK.
YEAH, YEAH-- IN A MINUTE.
NO-- NOW.
IN A MINUTE.
MY BLADDER'S ABOUT TO BLOW LIKE MOUNT VESUVIUS AND--
--AND...
OH, CRAP.
IT WASN'T A DREAM... WAS IT?
IF ONLY IT WAS, BUDDY.

...WELCOME TO THE *THIRTY-FIRST CENTURY!*

AS FUTURES *GO*-- THIS ONE'S KINDA *DISGUSTING.*

KEEP IN MIND THAT *TAKRON-GALTOS* IS A *PRISON PLANET.* YOU'RE NOT EXACTLY SEEING US AT OUR *BEST.*

SO THE *REST* OF THE UNIVERSE IS IN BETTER SHAPE THAN *THIS* HELLHOLE?

HONESTLY?

NOT *REALLY.*

WELL, BOOSTER, M'BOY-- LOOKS LIKE WE'VE *REALLY* SCREWED THE POOCH *THIS* TIME.

"SCREWED THE POOCH"? A 21ST CENTURY *COLLOQUIALISM?*

KIND OF OUR *MOTTO.*

JUSTICE LEAGUE 3000 featuring blue beetle & BOOSTER GOLD

ANOTHER FINE MESS!

They said it couldn't be done, but those knuckleheads*
KEITH GIFFEN, J.M. DEMATTEIS & HOWARD PORTER *did it anyway!*

HI-FI *colors* **ROB LEIGH** *letters* **BRIAN CUNNINGHAM** *group editor* **HARVEY RICHARDS** *editor* **PORTER & HI-FI** *cover*

*ACTUALLY, THEY SAID IT *SHOULDN'T* BE DONE. BUT DO THOSE GUYS EVER LISTEN? *NO!*

SO...uh...ANYWAY, SHERIFF TARIQ-- YOU SAY YOU FOUND US BURIED?
CONSTRUCTION CREW FOUND YOU--
--LOCKED UP TIGHT IN A PAIR OF OUTDATED, BARELY FUNCTIONING CRYOGENIC CRYPTS.
WHAT THE HELL WERE WE DOING IN THOSE?
I WAS HOPING YOU TWO COULD EXPLAIN THAT.
I WISH WE COULD. LAST THING I REMEMBER IS--
Huh. I THINK I WAS DRUNK.
BUT YOU DON'T DRINK.
I DON'T... DO I?
WHAT'S THE LAST THING YOU REMEMBER?
WE WERE HAVING A SURPRISE BIRTHDAY PARTY FOR RALPH-- AND MAX WAS YELLING AT US BECAUSE--
WELL, BECAUSE HE WAS MAX.
AND THEN?
THEN IT ALL STARTS TO GET HAZY.
BUT YOUR WORLD... YOUR ERA... YOU REMEMBER THAT WELL ENOUGH?
Uh-huh. WHY?
SO MUCH OF OUR HISTORY HAS BEEN LOST. YOU TWO COULD PROVE TO BE INVALUABLE SOURCES OF INFORMATION.
ARE THERE ANY SURVIVING RECORDS ABOUT US?
MINIMAL. SOMETHING ABOUT A VIGILANTE GROUP CALLED THE--SUPER BUDDIES...?
NOT VIGILANTES: HEROES. AND WE WERE PART OF THE J.L.I. BEFORE THAT.
J.L.I.?
JUSTICE LEAGUE INTERNATIONAL.
JUSTICE LEAGUE? INTERESTING.
LOOK-- WE NEED A LITTLE TIME TO DIGEST ALL THIS AND--
TAKE ALL THE TIME YOU NEED. YOU KNOW WHERE TO FIND ME. AND PLEASE... FOR YOUR OWN SAFETY--

WOULDN'T *THINK* OF IT!
Uh...IS HE *GONE?*
YEAH.
THEN *COME ON--*
WHERE?
WE'RE GETTING THE HELL *OUT* OF HERE.
BUT THE *SHERIFF* JUST SAID--
SINCE WHEN DO *YOU* TRUST AUTHORITY FIGURES?
IT'S NOT *ABOUT* THAT! WE JUST WOKE UP A *THOUSAND YEARS* FROM THE NEAREST *STARBUCKS!*
YOU'RE *USED* TO GALLIVANTING ACROSS THE CENTURIES!
ME? I NEED A MONTH OR TWO TO COLLECT MY *BRAIN CELLS* AND--
DON'T YOU FIND IT ODD THAT THE SHERIFF ON A *PRISON PLANET* DIGS UP TWO *RANDOM* SLEEPERS-- AND TREATS THEM LIKE *HONORED GUESTS?*
FOR ALL WE KNOW, THIS TARIQ IS THE ONE RESPONSIBLE FOR *BRINGING* US HERE!
Y WOULD HE DO *THAT?*
THAT'S WHAT WE'VE GOT TO *FIND OUT.*
AY, *I'M IN--* CAN WE GET *REAKFAST* FIRST?
FOOD? *SERIOUSLY?*
HEY--I HAVEN'T HAD A MEAL IN *TEN CENTURIES* AND, WITH MY *HYPOGLYCEMIA*...WELL--
YOU KNOW HO *BITCHY* I CAN WHEN I HAVEN *EATEN.*
HEART CONDITION, REMEMBER?
sigh I DO *INDEED.*
C'MON-- LET'S SEE IF WE CAN FIND YOU THE THIRTY-FIRST CENTURY EQUIVALENT OF *BACON* AND *EGGS.*

"IT'S SOY BACON IN A TOFU SCRAMBLE FOR ME!"
YOU'RE JUST LETTING THEM ROAM FREE?
THE ENTIRE PLANET IS A PRISON, TERRY. THEY'RE HARDLY FREE.
CADMUS
CADMUSWORLD...

BESIDES--I'M THERE... IN MULTIPLE BODIES... WATCHING THEM AT ALL TIMES.
AND YOU'VE NEVER BUNGLED A JOB BEFORE--HAVE YOU, CONVERT?
WHAT HAPPENED BACK ON CAMELOT NINE WASN'T MY FAULT!
REALLY? THE REBORN JUSTICE LEAGUE DEFEATED THE FIVE! HUMILIATED US AND--

ACH! NO REASON TO KEEP GOING OVER IT. AS FOR THIS...BEAGLE AND BUSTER--
BEETLE AND BOOSTER.
WHATEVER. I DON'T SEE THEIR VALUE. THEY DON'T EVEN POSSESS ANY METAHUMAN ABILITIES.

CARBON DATING AND A BATTERY OF BIOSCANS CONFIRMS THEY'RE GENUINE SURVIVORS FROM THE TWENTY-FIRST CENTURY.
A LIVING LINK TO THE PAST. KNOWLEDGE--AS YOU KNOW BETTER THAN MOST--IS POWER.
DO WHAT YOU WANT WITH THEM. I'M STILL PREPPING MY INJUSTICE LEAGUE AND I CAN'T BE BOTHERED WITH--

DID I FORGET TO MENTION THAT MY TWO SLEEPERS WERE ONCE MEMBERS OF THE--
--JUSTICE LEAGUE INTERNATIONAL?

YOU HAVE ONE WEEK TO STUDY THEM--THEN I WANT THEM HERE AT CADMUS, WHERE I'LL INTERROGATE THEM--

"--PERSONALLY."
AMAZING! SOME OF THIS STILL LOOKS LIKE OUR TIME. BUT WHAT THE HELL HAPPENED TO TURN THE UNIVERSE UPSIDE DOWN LIKE THIS?
HOW SHOULD I KNOW?
HOW SHOULD--?!
YOU'RE A TIME TRAVELER FROM A FUTURE BEYOND THIS ONE! YOU SHOULD KNOW ALL ABOUT THIS STUFF!
YEAH, WELL, MAYBE I WAS ABSENT THE DAY WE COVERED THE EARLY THIRTY-FIRST CENTURY!
TOO BAD SKEETS ISN'T HERE.
LAST I CHECKED, YOUR LITTLE ROBOT PAL WAS IN YOUR CLOSET... DEACTIVATED--
KOOL KOLA
KATS
SUBWAY
REGALY BLOM
CHICKGO
--AND BURIED UNDER YOUR PORN COLLECTION.
NOT PORN... EROTICA!
HEY, I SOLD IT TO YOU AND I SAY IT'S PORN!
LOOK, BEETLE--I KNOW YOU'RE WORRIED. I'M WORRIED, TOO.
BUT WE'LL GET OUT OF THIS-- THE WAY WE'VE GOTTEN OUT OF EVERY OTHER MESS WE'VE FOUND OURSELVES IN.
DUMB LUCK?
I'LL GET US HOME. I PROMISE.
WHY AM I NOT REASSURED?
THEY BICKER LIKE CHILDREN.

AN' WE GIVE A CRAP ABOUT THOSE TWO *BECAUSE...?*
TAKE A CLOSER *LOOK.*
TAKE A CLOSER--?
HEY! WHY'S THAT GUY WEARIN' A SUIT LIKE *MINE?*
ACTUALLY-- *YOU'RE* THE ONE IMITATING *HIM!*
WHAT THE HELL ARE YOU *TALKIN'* ABOUT, *CONVERT?*
HAVEN'T YOU EVER WONDERED WHERE YOUR UNIFORM... YOUR EQUIPMENT... *CAME* FROM?
MY FATHER *FOUND* IT--EXCAVATING SOME RUINS DOWNTOWN. *DUMBASS* COULDN'T FIGURE OUT WHAT TO *DO* WITH THE STUFF--
--BUT *I* WAS THE GUY WITH THE BRAINS TO--
SMEK
TO RUN AROUND A *PRISON WORLD*--TRYING TO CAPTURE *CRIMINALS?*
HEY...YOU GOT PEOPLE TRYIN' TO BUST OUTTA THE CONDOS ALL THE *TIME!* IF IT WASN'T FOR *ME--*
LOOK--WE'VE HAD NO PROBLEM LETTING YOU *RUN FREE* HERE ON T.K. IT'S BEEN AMUSING--AND EVEN *HELPFUL,* ON OCCASION.
BUT *LEAVE THOSE TWO ALONE.*
THEY DON'T BREAK NO *RULES,* THEY DON'T GET *HASSLED.* BUT I'M

"--I DON'T LIKE THAT SKINNY LITTLE SHMUCK RUNNIN' AROUND IN MY COSTUME!"
...THAT'S THE THIRD CAFETERIA THEY THREW US OUT OF.
BOUND T' HAPPEN WHEN YOU DON'T HAVE ANY MONEY TO PAY WITH.
GOOD THING I SWIPED THOSE BAGS OF "PROTEIN KRUNCHIES," huh?
TASTED LIKE FREEZE-DRIED BARF--BUT AT LEAST IT GOT MY BLOOD SUGAR UP.
ENOUGH ABOUT YOUR DAMN BLOOD SUGAR!
WE'VE GOT TO FIND SOMEPLACE TO GO TO GROUND TILL I CAN FIGURE OUT A WAY TO GET US OFF THIS WORLD--
--OR BACK TO THE--
SOMETHING WRONG...?
YOU HAVE THE FEELING WE'RE... BEING WATCHED?
WE'RE IN A CITY THAT'S A JAIL! OF COURSE WE'RE BEING WATCHED! EVERYONE'S BEING WATCHED!
NOW, C'MON--
WHERE?
WHILE YOU'VE BEEN TALKING ABOUT AN ESCAPE PLAN... I ACTUALLY CAME UP WITH ONE!
YOU HAVE A PLAN? OH, COME NOW!
KORD INDUSTRIES HAD OFFICES IN A DOZEN CITIES ACROSS THE WORLD...RIGHT... INCLUDING NEW YORK?
SO?
SO--HALF A MILE BENEATH EACH OF THOSE OFFICES WAS A LITTLE HIDEAWAY WHERE I STASHED ALL MY EXTRA TECH.
TECH WE CAN USE TO MAKE OUR ESCAPE.
TED--IT'S BEEN A THOUSAND YEARS.
CAN'T HURT TO LOOK, CAN IT?
THE LAST TIME YOU SAID THAT WE--
NEVER GONNA LET ME FORGET THAT--

"--ARE YOU?"
I CAN'T BELIEVE WE WERE GIVEN A CASTLE!
I CAN'T BELIEVE WE ACCEPTED IT.
AMELOT NINE...
WHY ARE YOU BEING SO NEGATIVE, BATMAN? THIS IS AN AMAZING OPPORTUNITY FOR US.
I AGREE WITH TERI--
--A HEADQUARTERS IS JUST WHAT TEAM SUPERMAN NEEDS!
YEAH. JUSTICE LEAGUE IS SO TWENTY-FIRST CENTURY. FIGURED WE COULD USE A NAME WITH SOME SNAP...SOME SPARKLE.
TEAM SUPERMAN?
AND WITH ALL THE POSSIBILITIES AVAILABLE--YOU CAME UP WITH TEAM SUPERMAN?
AM I BRILLIANT-- OR WHAT?
FORGET IT, CLARK. THE NAME IS JUSTICE LEAGUE. IT'S WHO WE ARE. IT'S WHAT WE STAND FOR.
I DO HAVE ONE RESERVATION ABOUT THIS PLACE, THOUGH--
WHAT'S THAT, G.L.?
IT WAS GENEROUS OF KING ARTHUR TO LET US SET UP SHOP HERE, BUT--GIVEN OUR ENEMIES--DOESN'T OUR PRESENCE ON THIS PLANET--
--ENDANGER HIS ENTIRE KINGDOM?
PLEASE! ARTHUR'S ALREADY AT WAR WITH ETRIGAN'S DEMON EMPIRE. WHAT COULD BE MORE DANGEROUS THAN THAT?
ARIEL'S RIGHT-- SO LET'S NOT LOOK A GIFT CASTLE IN THE MOUTH.
HEY--WHERE'S DIANA? HOW COME SHE GETS TO GOOF OFF WHILE WE'RE ALL REMODELING?
DI'S BEEN A LITTLE... TENSE LATELY--SO ARTHUR GAVE HER PERMISSION TO JOIN HIS TROOPS IN DEMON TERRITORY--

"--AND LET OFF SOME STEAM."

"SO THIS IS KORD INDUSTRIES' *NEW YORK OFFICE?*"

GUESS IT'S SEEN BETTER DAYS, huh?
WELL, AS HOLES IN THE GROUND GO-- IT'S PRETTY IMPRESSIVE.
DOESN'T MEAN MY HIDDEN BUNKER'S NOT DOWN THERE. IT WAS BUILT TO LAST.
YOU'RE NOT REALLY GONNA--?
'COURSE I AM! AND YOU'RE COMING WITH ME!
AND WHY WOULD I DO THAT?
HEY! NOT ALL MY IDEAS HAVE BEEN MORONIC--
--AND I'VE DONE THE SAME FOR YOU.
--EXACTLY.
LOOK, IF THERE'S EVEN A CHANCE THAT MY SPARE BUG IS STILL DOWN THERE.
SPARE BUG?
MY ARMORED AND WEAPONIZED AIRSHIP...?
I KNOW WHAT IT IS! I JUST CAN'T BELIEVE YOU HAD MORE THAN ONE OF THEM!
ALWAYS HELPS TO HAVE AN EXTRA IN CASE OF EMERGENCIES.
BUT DIDN'T THAT COST A FORTUNE?
DON'T FORGET-- I WAS A WEALTHY MAN--
--ONCE.
RIGHT. AND YOU INHERITED ALL THAT LOOT FROM YOUR DADDY.

UNLIKE YOU--WHO MARRIED INTO IT.
I MARRIED GLADYS FOR LOVE. THE FACT THAT SHE WAS WEALTHY BEYOND MY WILDEST DREAMS HAD NOTHING TO DO WITH IT!
WELL... ALMOST NOTHING.

OKAY--SO IT HAD EVERYTHING TO DO WITH IT!
I DON'T LIKE THIS.
I DON'T LIKE THIS AT ALL.

SO HOW, EXACTLY, IS FINDING YOUR BUG GONNA HELP US?
WELL, IF IT'S INTACT--
WHICH IS A VERY BIG "IF"!
--I MIGHT BE ABLE TO MAKE SOME MODIFICATIONS...USE HER TO GET US OFF THE PLANET.
UNLESS YOU CAN TURN HER INTO A TIME MACHINE--I DON'T SEE HOW THAT'S GONNA HELP.

WE'RE A THOUSAND YEARS IN THE FUTURE... ALONE IN A HOSTILE UNIVERSE. WHERE THE HELL ARE WE GONNA GO?
THERE'S GOTTA BE SOME NICE LITTLE WORLD OUT THERE--
--PREFERABLY ONE FILLED WITH BEAUTIFUL WOMEN--
--WHERE WE CAN LIE LOW AND--
HEY! WHERE'S YOUR FLIGHT RING?

IT'S GONE!
MUST'VE BEEN TAKEN BEFORE I WOKE UP!
I'LL BET IT WAS THAT SHERIFF TARIQ! I TOLD YOU I DIDN'T TRUST HIM! HE--

DON'T MOVE!
"HE DON'T MOVE"? WHAT'S THAT SUPPOSED TO MEAN?
NO, YOU IDIOT! LOOK AROUND! THE TUNNEL--
--IT'S BEEN BOOBY-TRAPPED! ANOTHER STEP AND--
WOW. YOU SAVED MY LIFE, BOOSTER. GRACIAS.
THANK ME AFTER I DEACTIVATE THIS STUFF.
CAN YOU? I MEAN, THIS IS FUTURE TECH AND--
--AND I'M FROM THE FUTURE, REMEMBER? JUST A MINOR ADJUSTMENT AND--
--DONE!
T WE'VE LL GOT BE VERY AREFUL OR--
CAREFUL, SHMAREFUL!
TAKE A LOOK AT THAT, BUDDY!
MY STUFF! ALL MY BEAUTIFUL STUFF!
AND THERE'S OUR TICKET OUT OF HERE--LOOKING AS GOOD AS THE DAY I BUILT HER!
BEFORE YOU THROW A PARTY AND INVITE ALL OUR FRIENDS--
WHO, I MIGHT ADD, HAVE BEEN DEAD FOR CENTURIES.
--YOU MIGHT TRY TURNING IT ON.

DON'T WORRY! THIS BUG'LL FLY AND--
Hmmmmm.
"Hmmmmm" WHAT?
SOMEONE'S UPGRADED HER. NOT FOND OF THE NEW LOOK...BUT I GUESS IT'S THE THOUGHT THAT COUNTS.
MUST BE THE SAME SOMEONE--

--WHO BOOBY-TRAPPED THE TUNNEL. AND HE'S BEEN HERE RECENTLY.
HOW D'YA KNOW?
NO DUST. ANYWHERE.

IT'S ALL SPIT AND POLISH INSIDE, TOO!
WOW. THIS GUY REALLY DID A JOB ON THE UPHOLSTERY AND--
HEY! CHECK IT OUT!

MY AUTOGRAPHED PICTURE OF SUPERMAN IS STILL HERE! LAMINATED AND EVERYTHING!
To Blue Beetle... The bravest man I've ever known... Your Pal, Superman
"TO BLUE BEETLE...THE BRAVEST MAN I'VE EVER KNOWN...YOUR PAL, SUPERMAN."
YOU SIGNED THAT YOURSELF... DIDN'T YOU?
AS I RECALL-- I SIGNED ONE FOR YOU, TOO!

GIVEN WHAT WE'VE SEEN, IT'S SAFE TO ASSUME--
--THAT OUR MYSTERY MAN'S BEEN USING ALL THIS ON A REGULAR BASIS.
WELL, WHOEVER HE IS--HE OWES ME A BOATLOAD OF ROYALTIES.

I OWE YOU NOTHIN'-- YA STINKIN', IMPOSTOR!

THERE'S ONLY ROOM FOR *ONE BLUE BEETLE* IN THIS CITY--
I THINK HE MEANS *YOU.*
Blue Beetle- The bravest man I've ever known... Your Pal, Superman
SNA-KLANK
SNA-KLANK
--AND I'M IT!

HOW THE HELL DID HE SQUEEZE INTO MY COSTUME?
KANG
HE'S GOTTA WEIGH TWO HUNDRED POUNDS!
TO BE FAIR, I SEEM TO RECALL YOU GOING THROUGH A PUDGY PHASE AND--
TANG
WAIT A MINUTE! WHY THE HELL ARE WE EVEN TALKING ABOUT THIS?
TO DISTRACT US FROM THE UNSETTLING FACT THAT WE'RE GOING TO DIE, OF COURSE!
WE'RE NOT GOING TO DIE! SOON AS I TURN ON MY FORCE-FIELD, WE'LL--
Uh-oh.
TOMP
THEY TOOK THAT, TOO...DIDN'T THEY?
YEP.
WHAT'S THE PLAN NOW?
HIT HIM!
A LOT! AND THEN--
SMAK

--RUN AWAY!
WHAT'RE YOU *TALKING* ABOUT? YOU'RE A *BIGGER COWARD* THAN *I* AM!
I AM *NOT* RUNNING AWAY!
THAT WALKING PIECE OF OVERSTUFFED SPANDEX HAS GOT MY *STUFF*--
--AND I'M *GETTING IT BACK!*
NOW *LET GO* OF ME!
FOR CRYING OUT *LOUD,* TED--
--LOOK AT HIS *TECH!* HE'S GOT US *OUTGUNNED!*
NOT *HIS* TECH! *MY* TECH! *MINE!*
MAYBE IT WAS YOURS *ONCE,* DAFFY-- NOT *ANYMORE!*

RARRRCH RARRRCH
RARRRCH RARRRCH
WHAT'S THAT?
SOUNDS LIKE RATS-- SOMEWHERE IN THOSE TUNNELS BACK THERE.
IF YOU THINK I'M LETTING A FEW RATS--
--NO MATTER HOW CREEPY AND DISGUSTING--
--STOP ME FROM GETTING MY STUFF BACK--
YOU'RE NOT THINKING THIS THROUGH, BUDDY. THIS PLANET'S POLLUTED WAY BEYOND ANYTHING FROM YOUR TIME.
THERE'S TOXICITY EVERYWHERE. WHICH MEANS MUTATIONS--
--ARE A VERY DISTINCT POSSIBILITY!
RARRRCH RARRRCH RARRRCH
Y'KNOW THAT IDEA YOU HAD ABOUT RUNNING AWAY? IT'S STARTING TO SOUND AWFULLY GOOD TO--
--ME.
SO MUCH FOR DOUBLING BACK THE OTHER WAY.
KA-TANNNGG

RARRRCH
RARRRCH
~sigh~ SCREWED THE POOCH AGAIN--
--DIDN'T WE?
RARRRCH
RARRRCH
RARRRCH
RARRRCH

More adventure and absurdity in the 31st Century courtesy of: KEITH GIFFEN, J.M. DEMATTEIS & HOWARD PORTER

HI-FI colors | ROB LEIGH letters | BRIAN CUNNINGHAM group editor | HARVEY RICHARDS editor | PORTER & HI-FI cover

WELL, WE SOMEHOW ENDED UP IN SUSPENDED ANIMATION, AND WOKE UP ON A PRISON PLANET A THOUSAND YEARS IN THE FUTURE--
--AFTER WHICH WE CAME DOWN HERE TO THIS OLD BUNKER OF MINE LOOKING FOR SOME EQUIPMENT TO GET US OFF THIS HELLHOLE--
--AND RAN INTO MUTATED RATS AND A MAJOR LOON IN A BLUE BEETLE COSTUME WHO WANTS TO KILL US!
IT WAS A RHETORICAL QUESTION.
OH.
DON'T WASTE YOUR TIME WITH HIM! WE'VE GOT TO GET BACK TO THE SURFACE!
AND THEN WHAT?
THEN I'M GETTING US BACK TO OUR OWN CENTURY!
RARRRGH
RARRRGH
RARRRGH
RARRRGH
AND HOW DO YOU PROPOSE TO DO THAT?
I'M NOT SURE.
"I'M NOT SURE" DOESN'T EXACTLY QUALIFY AS AN ESCAPE STRATEGY!
YOU HAVE A BETTER IDEA?
YEAH! I GET MY BUG BACK FROM FAT-BOY OVER THERE...I MODIF IT FOR SPACE-TRAVEL--

--AND WE USE IT TO FLY US TO A FRIENDLY PLANET WHERE WE CAN LIE LOW FOR A WHILE!
YOU LEFT OUT THE PART WHERE WE'RE EATEN BY RATS!
NO, NO-- YOU'RE EATEN BY RATS!
I LIVE TO A RIPE OLD AGE AMONG PRIMITIVE-BUT-KINDLY ALIENS WHO WORSHIP ME AS A GOD!
BUT I PROMISE-- BOOSTER, OLD BUDDY-- THAT I'LL NEVER FORGET YOU!
KROOM
I CAN'T TELL YOU HOW MUCH I APPRECIATE THAT.
Uh...Y'THINK MAYBE YOU CAN HELP ME OUT HERE...?
SOON AS I'M DONE TAKING BACK WHAT'S MINE!
YOURS? YOU'RE NOTHIN' BUT A LOUSY IMPOSTOR!
I'M THE REAL BLUE BEETLE!
TED...? HELP...?
IF I GET RABIES, I SWEAR

BE RIGHT WITH YA, BUDDY--
--Y'KNOW, IF I CAN FIGURE OUT HOW TO WORK THESE CONTROLS!
YOU DESIGNED THE DAMN THING!
YEAH, BUT TUBBY THERE RE-DESIGNED IT AND I CAN'T--
ZATATATATATATATATATA
WHOA. GOOD SHOOTING, BEETLE!
IT WASN'T ME!
THEN WHO?
HIM. OUR...ah... GOOD BUDDY SHERIFF TARIQ--
WHO SEEMS TO RECALL TELLING YOU TWO IDIOTS NOT TO STRAY TOO FAR FROM THE COMPOUND!
HEY-- Y'CAN'T BLAME US FOR WANTING TO HAVE A LOOK AROUND.
NO. BUT I CAN BLAME YOU FOR WANTING TO ESCAPE.
YOU WERE WATCHING US THE WHOLE TIME-- WEREN'T YOU?
Uh-huh.
AND YOU NEARLY LET ME GET DEVOURED BY MUTANT VERMIN BECAUSE--?
BECAUSE I WANTED YOU TO UNDERSTAND JUST HOW DANGEROUS TAKRON-GALTOS IS.

I THINK YOU MADE YOUR POINT.
NOW WOULD YOU CARE TO EXPLAIN WHO HE IS?
NAME'S ELTON KOOKABURRA. HIS FATHER WAS A CONTRACTOR.
FOUND YOUR BUNKER AN' ALL YOUR TECH WHEN HE WAS EXCAVATING THESE RUINS.
YEAH--FOUND IT AND DIDN'T KNOW WHAT THE HELL T'DO WITH IT! BUT I DID!
AN' NOW ALL THIS STUFF IS MINE, Y'HEAR ME--AN' NO ONE'S TAKIN' IT AWAY!
HE'S ACTUALLY HELPED US OUT ON OCCASION...BRINGING IN RUNNERS WHEN THEY TRY TO ESCAPE THE CITY--
--BUT MOSTLY HE'S JUST A HUGE PAIN IN THE ASS.
I'M SURPRISED HE DIDN'T TRY TO SELL IT ALL OFF.
OH, HE DID. NOBODY WANTED ANY OF THIS JUNK.
IN CASE YOU MISSED IT, HE JUST CALLED YOUR LIFE'S WORK JUNK.
NO OFFENSE. BUT, EVEN WITH ELTON'S MODIFICATIONS--
--THIS STUFF IS TOTALLY OUT OF DATE.
I AM VENGEANCE! I AM THE NIGHT! I'M THE FRICKIN' BLUE BEETLE!
AND THE LEGEND LIVES ON.
OH, GOD, I'M SO EMBARRASSED.
OKAY, YOU TWO, COME ON--BACK TO THE COMPOUND!

"WE NEED TO HAVE A LITTLE TALK."
CAMELOT NINE...
BUT I'VE FINISHED THE CONSTRUCTION ON THE TRAINING CENTER AND THE MONITOR ROOM AND--
FINISHED? BUT YOU JUST LEFT HERE THREE MINUTES AGO.
ARIEL...?
NOT NOW, TERI.
FASTEST WOMAN ALIVE... REMEMBER?
WELL, THEN, TAKE A BREAK WHILE I FINISH CALIBRATING THESE OMNIPUTERS AND--
I CAN'T TAKE A BREAK!
SINCE YOU SPLICED MY D.N.A. WITH BARRY ALLEN'S I HAVEN'T BEEN ABLE TO SLEEP...MY THOUGHTS HAVE BEEN RACING SO FAST I CAN HARDLY KEEP UP WITH THEM--
--ANDIFI'MNOT CONSTANTLYDOING SOMETHINGANDDOING ITQUICKLYISTARTTO FEELLIKEI'MGOING TOJUMPOUT OFMY--
TERI-- TAKE IT EASY!
I WOULD IF I COULD!
IT'S NOT GOING TO STAY THIS WAY. YOUR BODY'S ADJUSTING TO ITS NEW D.N.A. MATRIX. OVER THE NEXT FEW DAYS--
--YOUR BIOLOGY WILL REACH A NEW BALANCE AND--
WELLWHATAM ISUPPOSEDTODOWHILEI'MWAITING? IT'SLIKETHEWHOLEWORLD'SSLOWED DOWN!ICANHARDLYSTANDSTILL ANDHAVEACONVERSATIONWITH--
WELL--WE HAVEN'T HEARD FROM WONDER WOMAN IN A WHILE. WHY DON'T YOU GO CHECK ON--

I'M ON IT!
FLONK
BLONK
KONK
A WOMAN WHO MOVES FASTER THAN THE WIND? THESE NEWCOMERS FRIGHTEN ME, BRUNNHILDE.
EVERYTHING FRIGHTENS YOU, HANS!
OH, YOU SHOULD BE FRIGHTENED-- YOU IGNORANT, UNWASHED PEASANT...
...BUT NOT OF HER.
AS FAR AS I CAN TELL, THIS RESURRECTED JUSTICE LEAGUE IS A JOKE... AND I'LL TAKE THEM DOWN IN THIS CENTURY AS EASILY AS I DID IN THE LAST.
SO BE AFRAID, PEASANT--BUT NOT OF THEM. OF ME.

LOIS LANE.
I CANNOT FAULT YOUR SKILL IN BATTLE, LADY DIANA.
NOR I YOURS, SIR AGLOVALE. AND IT'S JUST DIANA. I ASSURE YOU--

--I'M NO LADY.
PERHAPS NOT... IN THE COURTLY SENSE...BUT YOU ARE ALL WOMAN.
FORGIVE ME. THAT WAS AN... UNSEEMLY THING TO SAY.
NOT AT ALL. I LIKE YOU, AGLOVALE-- AND, WHEN WE'RE DONE GUTTING DEMONS, I LOOK FORWARD TO SEVERAL NIGHTS OF... UNSEEMLY PURSUITS.
SPEAKING OF DEMONS--
--WHY HAVE WE LEFT ETRIGAN'S TERRITORY--AND MARCHED OUT TO THESE GODFORSAKEN WASTES?
WE CALL IT THE FROZEN REACH--
--AND THERE'S AT LEAST ONE GOD WHO HASN'T FORSAKEN IT.
WHAT DO YOU MEAN?
COME...LET ME SHOW YOU.
ARE YOU SERIOUS ABOUT THERE BEING GODS HERE?
A GODDESS, ACTUALLY--
--AND SHE MAY PROVE VITAL IN OUR WAR AGAINST ETRIGAN'S ARMIES.
IT'S BEEN A LONG CAMPAIGN, HASN'T IT?
MORE YEARS THAN I'D CARE TO COUNT-- AND WE'VE LOST FAR TOO MANY GOOD MEN AND WOMEN IN THE FIGHT.

BUT IF WE CAN PERSUADE THE ICE GODDESS TO JOIN OUR CAUSE--
ICE GODDESS...? WHAT'S HER NAME?
THAT I DO NOT KNOW. SHE WAS IMPRISONED BY ETRIGAN--LONG AGO--BUT NOW THAT OUR FORCES HAVE BEEN ABLE TO PUSH DEEPER INTO THE DEMON-LORD'S KINGDOM--
--WE FINALLY HAVE ANOTHER CHANCE TO REACH HER CASTLE AND SET HER FREE.
THERE!
THEY SAY SHE SLEEPS WITHIN THOSE VERY WALLS!
"THEY SAY"? YOU DON'T KNOW FOR SURE?
NO.
THEN THIS COULD BE A TRAP! WE MIGHT BE--
DIANA!
A SPEED DEMON! STAND BACK, DIANA, WHILE I--
PUT THE SWORD AWAY, AGLOVALE--
--SHE'S ONE OF MY PEOPLE.
SORT OF.
WAIT? ARE YOU SAYING THAT THERE ARE ACTUALLY SPEED DEMONS?
AND DEADLY BEASTS THEY ARE, M'LADY.
NEVER MIND THAT. WHAT ARE YOU DOING HERE?
WHAT'S CLARK DONE NOW?
NO, NO--EVERYTHING'S FINE. ARIEL JUST WANTED ME TO CHECK UP ON YOU.

NO! THAT'S NOT WHAT SHE--
OR MAYBE IT WAS.
WHATEVER. ATLEASTITGOTMEOUTOF THECASTLE. IWASGOING STIRCRAZYTHERE. THIS NEWD.N.A. HASGOTME--
THAT?
OUR OBJECTIVE. AND IT SUDDENLY OCCURS TO ME THAT YOU CAN REACH IT FAR MORE QUICKLY THAN THE REST OF US.
WAIT. ME? ALONE? WH-WHAT'S IN THERE?
EITHER AN ANCIENT GODDESS OR A HORDE OF DEMONS OUT FOR BLOOD.
HOLD ON! I'M NEW AT THIS SUPER-HERO THING! THERE'S NO WAY I CAN--
YOU'RE A WOMAN OF INTELLIGENCE AND POWER, TERI. THERE'S NOTHING YOU CAN'T DO!
BUT... GODS AND DEMONS--?
WE'RE SENDING YOU TO SCOUT AND REPORT. MOVE FAST ENOUGH AND THEY WON'T EVEN KNOW YOU'RE THERE.
BUT--
YOU ARE NOT JUST ONE OF THE JUSTICE LEAGUE NOW, TERI--YOU ARE MY SISTER IN BATTLE! ALL MY FAITH, MY TRUST, MY HOPE--I PLACE IN YOU.
SISTERS? REALLY?
NOW AND FOREVER.
FWOOOSH
YOU DIDN'T MEAN A WORD OF THAT... DID YOU?
NO. BUT IT WORKED--

"--AND THAT'S ALL THAT MATTERS."
YOU SENT TERI WHERE?!
SHE'LL BE FINE.
WHAT WERE YOU THINKING? IF SHE RUNS INTO ETRIGAN'S FORCES, THEY'LL EAT HER ALIVE!
LITERALLY!
DON'T YOU THINK YOU'RE OVERREACTING...?
I AM NOT OVERREACTING! TERI'S A NOVICE! HELL...SHE'S JUST A CHILD--
--AND YOU JUST SENT THAT CHILD INTO THE PITS OF HELL!
SHE'S WITH DIANA--
WHO, AS WE ALL KNOW, IS THE SOUL OF CAUTION! IF ANYONE'S GONNA GET TERI KILLED, IT'S HER!
WHY DO YOU EVEN CARE? I THOUGHT THE ONLY PERSON YOU GAVE A DAMN ABOUT WAS YOURSELF.
YOU THOUGHT WRONG!
UP, UP AND--
--AWAY
DID I JUST SEE SUPERMAN JUMP OUT THE--?
YEP. POOR GUY. WHEN HE GETS EXCITED HE TENDS TO FORGET--
KEE-RASSSH

"--THAT HE *CAN'T FLY.*"

WHAT A *LIFE!* ONE MINUTE I'M A GIRL-GENIUS, RUNNING THE *CADMUS PROJECT* ALONGSIDE MY BROTHER, AND THE NEXT...HE *MURDERS* ME.

THEN ARIEL *RESURRECTS* ME AND TURNS ME INTO... *THIS.* NOT THAT SHE *ASKED.*

I'M *GRATEFUL* TO BE ALIVE--BUT I DON'T KNOW IF I'VE GOT WHAT IT TAKES TO STEP INTO *BARRY ALLEN'S SHOES.* HE WAS--

WAIT A MINUTE! WHAT'S THAT? *DEMONS! DOZENS* OF THEM...

...DID THIS?
THAT WOMAN-- UP THERE ON THE THRONE.
SHE'S AS FROZEN AS THE OTHERS--BUT EVEN STILL, THERE'S A FEELING OF GENTLENESS...AND MAJESTY...ABOUT HER.
YOU...YOU MUST BE THE GODDESS DIANA WAS TALKING ABOUT.
I NEVER DREAMED BEINGS LIKE YOU ACTUALLY EXISTED. AND NOW, HERE I AM-- FACE-TO-FACE WITH ONE!
I WONDER WHAT YOU'D SAY-- IF YOU WERE ALIVE. IF YOU COULD SPEAK.

I'D ASK YOU TO KEEP IT DOWN--
--BECAUSE YOU'RE DISTURBING MY NAP.
YOU'RE N-NOT DEAD?
MUCH AS I'D LIKE TO BE... NO. ONE OF THE DRAWBACKS OF IMMORTALITY.
NOW WHO ARE YOU--AND WHAT ARE YOU DOING IN MY CASTLE?
I...I... I...I...
FROZEN WITH FEAR, I SEE. AND WITH GOOD REASON.
ETRIGAN AND ARTHUR HAVE BOTH SENT THEIR PAWNS TO DRAW ME OUT--AND THEY'VE ALL PAID THE PRICE.
BUT I THOUGHT E-ETRIGAN IMPRISONED YOU HERE AND--
I IMPRISONED MYSELF. AND NOW, UNFORTUNATELY--
--IT'S TIME TO IMPRISON YOU.
PREPARE FOR THE WINTER OF THE SOUL, CHILD. IT WON'T HURT, I PROMISE YOU.
NOWWAIT AMINUTE--
--CAN'TWE TALKABOUTTHIS? I'MNOTYOUR ENEMY--
--IJUST CAMEHERETO SCOUTFOR DIANAAND--
WAIT. DID YOU SAY-- DIANA...?
HEY... YOU!

TAKE YOUR HANDS OFF THAT GIRL--
--BEFORE I CRACK YOU INTO A THOUSAND ICE CUBES!
SUPERMAN-- WAIT! I DON'T THINK SHE REALLY MEANS US ANY HARM! IF WE CAN JUST TALK TO HER--
TAKE A LOOK AROUND THIS CASTLE, KID--SHE MEANS EVERYONE HARM!
DID YOU CALL HIM... SUPERMAN?
YES!
BUT SUPERMAN...IS LONG DEAD.
I GOT BETTER!
DURING MY TRAINING, YOU TOLD ME THAT VIOLENCE SHOULD BE A LAST RESORT! THAT WE NEED TO EXPLORE EVERY POSSIBLE OPTION BEFORE--
YOU SHOULD EXPLORE EVERY POSSIBLE OPTION--NOT ME! PUNCHING AND HITTING IS WHAT I DO--
ENOUGH!
--BEST...!

THAT WON'T HOLD HIM VERY LONG.
LONG ENOUGH FOR YOU TO EXPLAIN WHAT'S GOING ON.
HOW CAN THAT POSSIBLY BE SUPERMAN? I WATCHED HIM DIE. I MOURNED HIM.
WAIT, WAIT-- YOU TWO KNOW EACH OTHER?
I'LL ASK THE QUESTIONS, CHILD--

--AND YOU'LL DO THE ANSWERING.
IT'S KIND OF A LONG STORY, BUT... HE IS SUPERMAN. THE ONE FROM A THOUSAND YEARS AGO--
--ONLY, WELL, HE'S NOT. I MEAN, IT'S HIS D.N.A....BUT SOMETHING WENT WRONG IN THE RESURRECTION PROCESS AND--

TRAITOR! YOU SHARE OUR SECRETS--WITH THE ENEMY?
Uh-oh. THERE GOES ANY CHANCE OF TALKING THIS THROUGH.
DIANA OF THEMYSCIRA?

IS IT TRULY YOU?
TORA? TORA OLAFSDOTTER?
OR AS THE JUSTICE LEAGUE ONCE CALLED ME-- ICE.
WHOA, WHOA, WHOA-- YOU WERE IN THE LEAGUE?

SHE WAS IN AN INCARNATION OF THE LEAGUE THAT MOST OF US WOULD LIKE TO FORGET.
THE JUSTICE LEAGUE INTERNATIONAL SERVED PROUDLY-- AND WELL!
AS BEST I REMEMBER-- THE J.L.I. WAS A JOKE!
ONLY TO AN ARROGANT, HUMORLESS OAF LIKE YOU!

HEY, HEY-- BOTH OF YOU BE NICE!
TORA...ICE... YOUR MAJESTY-- IF YOU WERE IN THE LEAGUE, THEN WE'RE ALL ON THE SAME SIDE HERE!
MY DAYS OF TAKING SIDES-- ARE LONG PAST. I BEG YOU, PLEASE GO--

"--AND LEAVE ME IN PEACE."
HOW LONG DO WE WAIT, SIR AGLOVALE?
UNTIL DIANA GIVES THE SIGNAL.
AND YOU TRUST HER?
SHE IS, AFTER ALL, A STRANGER IN OUR REALM AND--
SHE AND HER COMRADES ARE UNDER THE KING'S PROTECTION--AND DIANA HAS FOUGHT BESIDE US--
--MORE BRAVELY THAN THE FIERCEST OF ARTHUR'S KNIGHTS. SO YES, I TRUST HER--
--WITH MY LIFE!
AND THERE-- THE SIGNAL!
SHE WANTS US TO WAIT! THAT MEANS IT ISN'T ONE OF ETRIGAN'S TRAPS--
"--AND THE GODDESS IS FREE!"
SO YOU AGREE WITH ME...WE NEED TO TALK WITH ICE--NOT FIGHT...?
I REACTED INSTINCTIVELY... EMOTIONALLY...AS I OFTEN DO.
THE TRUTH IS-- WITH THE GAPS IN MY MEMORY--I DON'T REALLY REMEMBER ALL THAT MUCH ABOUT HER--
--BUT WE CLEARLY HAD OUR DIFFERENCES.
WELL, WHATEVER THEY WERE--IT WAS TEN CENTURIES AGO AND--
...YOU SURE THE TWO OF US NEVER MINGLED LIMBS?
OH, NO. HE'S OUT--

"--AND UP TO HIS *USUAL TRICKS!*"
YOU BESMIRCH THE MEMORY OF MY *TRUE LOVE* WITH YOUR *CRUDE INNUENDOS.*
OH, COME *ON*-- IF YOU KNEW ME BACK THEN, WE MUST HAVE TAKEN A TRIP TO *POUND TOWN* AT LEAST *ONCE.*
YOU ARE *NOT* THE SUPERMAN I REMEMBER.
NO--
--I'M *WAYYY* BETTER.
DOWN, CLARK. GIVE TORA *TIME* TO GET TO KNOW THE *NEW* YOU--
--SO SHE CAN *REALLY* BE REPULSED.
THAT WAS *MEAN.*
WASN'T IT?

HOW DO WE EVEN KNOW SHE'S THE *REAL* ICE? I MEAN, HOW DID SHE EVEN *LIVE* THIS LONG?
SHE'S AN *IMMORTAL!*
SO?
sigh I *GIVE UP!*
TORA...CAN WE DIAL THIS *BACK? START OVER* AGAIN?
TERI'S *RIGHT...* WE SHARE A *HISTORY.* WE SHOULD BE *ALLIES,* NOT *ENEMIES.*
I HAVE NEITHER ALLIES *NOR* ENEMIES. I HAVE ONLY *MYSELF.*
BUT I *AM* CURIOUS ABOUT HOW YOU CAME TO *BE* ON THIS WORLD... IN THIS *TIME*--

"A VERY COLD HELL."
THE GODDESS WEEPS AND WITH HER TEARS COME MEMORIES OF FALLEN YEARS!
OF COMRADES OLD! OF BATTLES FOUGHT! OF LOYALTIES SO LONG FORGOT!
AND THIS THE DEMON WON'T ABIDE! SHE CANNOT JOIN ARTHUR'S SIDE!
BUT ETRIGAN IS WISE AND CUNNING AND I'LL SOON HAVE THAT COLD BITCH RUNNING! I'LL ROAST HER 'PON AN ICY PYRE!
CALL THE WOMAN! BRING ME--
--FIRE!

JUSTICE LEAGUE 3000 SKETCHBOOK BY HOWARD PORTER

Scar

flight tech

Lois

Kirby new gods-ish

Zeus

Sinestro

Ugly
bōne

Pretty much Kirby
etrigan

MIRROR MASTER 3000

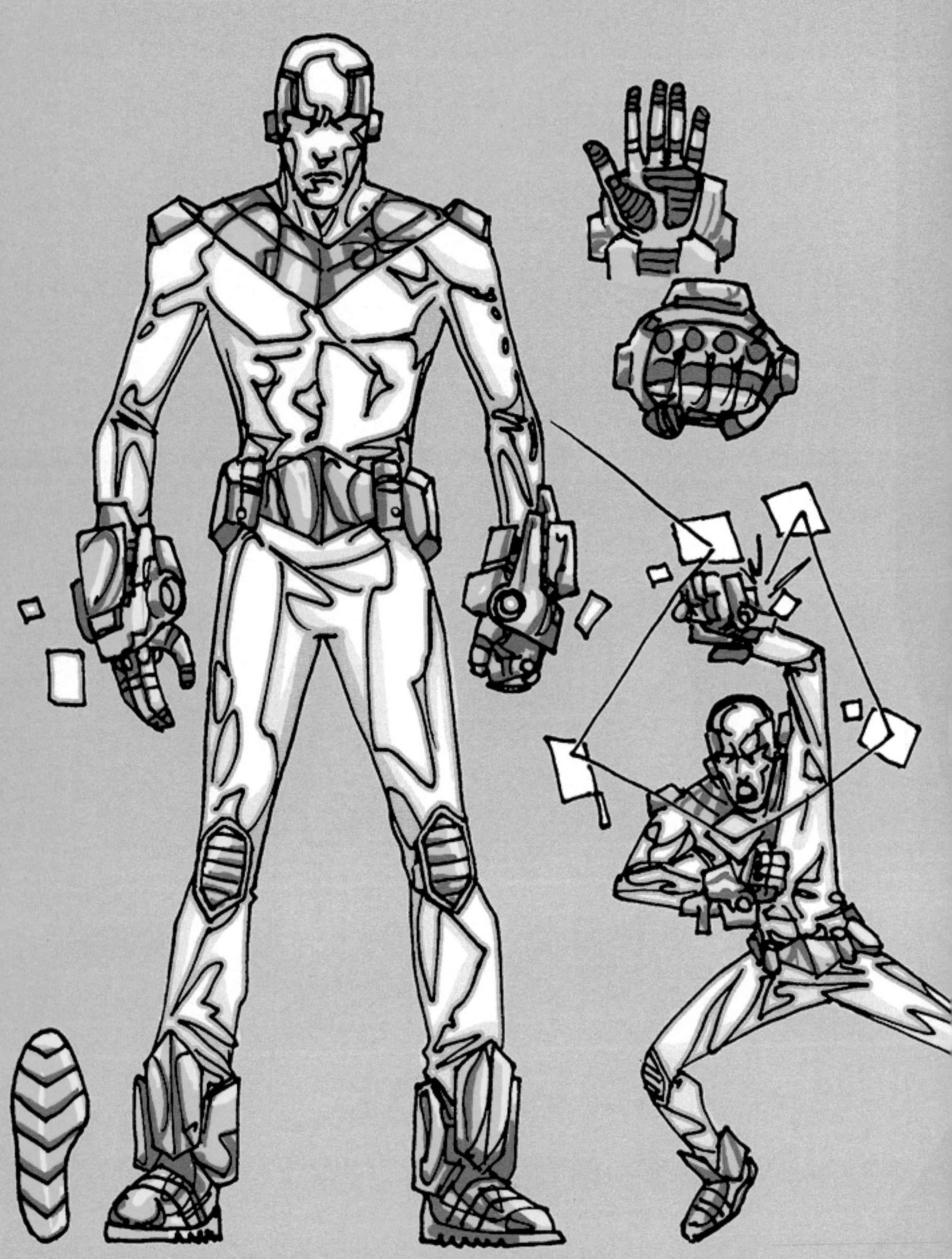

DESIGN BY SCOTT KOLINS